Living in Abundance

Exploring your worth,

the depth of God's love,

and His purpose for you.

Trish Kuhl

You are worthy. You are loved. You have purpose.

Living in Abundance

Exploring your worth, the depth of God's love, and His purpose for you.
Copyright © 2025 by Trish Kuhl.

For more information, email at tkuhl1962@gmail.com
Paperback ISBN: 979-8-9989810-0-5
Hardback ISBN: 979-8-9989810-1-2

Illustrations by: Michele Chitsey
Printed in the United States of America
Abundant Heart Publishing
Prairie Grove, Arkansas

DEDICATION

*This book is dedicated to the memory of Lisa Ann Wilhite,
the best miracle and sister ever.*

*My sweet Lisa, I dearly loved and admired you from the
moment Mom held you up to the hospital window while we
waited outside in the November cold, just to get a glimpse of
our baby sister.*

*God anointed you for His purpose. I am honored to have
watched you live out love, joy, peace, patience, kindness,
goodness, faithfulness, gentleness, and self-control. These
qualities were ingrained in your DNA. I never heard you
complain once, even through two battles of cancer.*

*As the older sister, I should have taught you. Graciously, the
Lord knew I needed to be taught by you. Thank you for being
my best friend, my confidant, my spiritual advisor, and so
much more, especially during your last months on earth.*

*I will always consider it a privilege to have witnessed your
beautiful life—a life that modeled God's unconditional love
and compassion to everyone.*

*My prayer is that I honor your legacy in remembering and
exemplifying the unconditional love and grace you showered
on others.*

*Until we meet again on those glorious streets of gold, you
will continue to be my hero.*

CONTENTS

ACKNOWLEDGMENTS

Nicole, I know without a doubt you are one of the best gifts God had waiting for me in my move to Arkansas. I can never repay your wisdom, kindness, and most of all, your genuine love for me. Your encouragement and continued "you can do it" words are the reason my dreams are coming true.

Maria, I'm almost embarrassed by the amount of support you provided me, both mentally and physically. Your daily prayers and steady guidance over my emotional well-being were a testament of what it means to be the hands and feet of Jesus. I would not have survived the rollercoaster of the past eighteen months without you and the strength God gave you to help me through the hard days and long sleepless nights. I also want to thank you for the countless hours of proofreading, editing, and suggestions that I mentioned from the beginning of this publishing process, you wouldn't need to do. *Sorry.* You are, without a doubt, my most outstanding achievement on this earth. God blessed me beyond measure, allowing me to be your mom. I love you, sweet girl.

Hannah McDonald, what a gift God bestowed on our family through you and your family. Maria was only able to support me so well because of the support you gave her. Your

1

constant prayers for Maria's family and me are pillars of strength supplied only by God. I pray the Lord will bless you and your family with more than an abundance of love, joy, peace, patience, kindness, goodness, faithfulness, gentleness, and self-control. You, my friend, are also an example of the hands and feet of Jesus. Saying thank you doesn't seem to be enough!

Michele Chitsey, thank you for accepting me and all my craziness. Your patience and creative talent have overflowed into my desire to write so others may be encouraged. I have no idea why God honored me with your friendship and made you the best writing partner, but I'm over the moon happy He did. Writing our first book together was more fun than I could have asked for or imagined. I love you and can't wait to see how God uses us again.

Nicole and Shana with ThriveIn Learning, thank you for the incredible experience of working with the ThriveIn team! I pray my appreciation shines through for the support and knowledge you've provided. Your commitment to helping new and experienced authors overcome fear and build confidence is invaluable. It's rare to find people who share their expertise and make such a tangible difference in someone else's dreams.

Alexa Follas, MA, CTRS, I thank God for intersecting our paths. I am beyond grateful for your loving guidance as my therapist. Your kindness, patience, and sincerity in my healing journey were undoubtedly orchestrated by God. Even more, I thank you for your friendship and your encouragement that reminds me I am worthy of a life lived in abundance—a life lived out loud for Christ. A life where I use my pain to help others.

Above all, I must thank God. Father, I praise You for rescuing me. It was only made possible by the Love You bestowed upon me by sending your son to die for my sins. I have no words to truly articulate my gratitude.

I am in awe of how You transformed situations I thought were hopeless, bringing them to glory in Your Holy name. Situations I thought I'd never survive are now ones that are more than I could have asked or imagined. You healed my heart in a way I never thought possible.

Even when others discouraged, dismissed, or misunderstood me, You helped me to use the tools You had already placed in my heart to love others for You and Your Kingdom.

May I always walk in the calling You designed for me (Ephesians 2:10), and live a life of abundance that will grow Your Kingdom.

FORWARD

Living in Abundance—what an amazing title for a Christian book! It immediately stirs hope and expectation. And yet, I know there will be those who find themselves feeling unsettled by the title. How do I know this? Because in one season of my life, I would have been that person—the one who said, *"Living in Abundance? Probably another prosperity gospel message with a bunch of fluff."* The me back then—jaded by church hurt and religion—would have been very, very wrong.

I have had the privilege of sitting with Trish, behind the scenes, as she worked through the ideas, outline, editing, and many tears it took to bring this book to you. Whether our talks were at vending events, coffee shops, or around kitchen tables, the message was always the same: *"I'm not sure why God has chosen me to deliver this message. I want to deliver it, but I feel unqualified. BUT I also know He doesn't call the qualified; He qualifies the called."* Amen, sister!

As Christians, I believe we can easily get ensnared by the lie that claiming abundant living is boastful—and many of us have been told over the years that being boastful is not a Christlike quality. Boasting in our own works is not Christlike at all. But I thank God that He is in the business of flipping the script, rewriting the story, and redeeming things—including words.

Paul confirms numerous times in the New Testament that it is good for believers to "boast in Christ". (2 Corinthians 12:9, Galatians 6:14, Philippians 1:26) And throughout the Old Testament, so many declared the very "boastful" statement: *"My God will prevail or provide."*

As you sit down to read this book, I pray you would ask God to help you set aside any tainted lenses you may have acquired over the years, any uncertainty about what God does and does not provide for His children, and any doubts about how much He lavishly loves you.

As Trish reminds us—and you will soon discover: You are loved. You are worthy. You have a purpose.

We are not meant to boast with pride in our own efforts and trust in our ability to take care of things. We were not placed here to seek self-indulgent abundance. We were created to accept the many unmerited gifts from the Father and live abundant lives overflowing with the fruit of the Spirit, so the world would see His good works in us and turn to Him.

Get ready to silence Satan's lies and turn up the volume on God's truth as you march into a life of **living in abundance!**

May your heart be opened wide and your spirit be refreshed as you read these pages.

I cannot wait to see what God does through the message within this book.

Blessed and honored to call Trish my friend,

Nicole Donoho

INTRODUCTION

"You cannot protect her." The fear that those four words unearthed in me led to a collapse on the kitchen floor and a car ride to my first therapy appointment.

It was a Sunday morning, and my family was outwardly ready for church. I say outwardly because on the inside, I wasn't ready for anything.

I fell to the kitchen floor, sobbing, no longer able to put one foot in front of the other.

The hidden secret that had lingered deep in my mind, heart, and soul for over 25 years was never intended to be brought to the surface.

However, with the birth of my beautiful daughter, a little over two years before the collapse to the floor, this secret that I had pushed down and protected ever so tightly resurfaced, and it did so with a vengeance. There was nothing I wanted more than to protect her. So, from the day she was born, I lived in fear that she would experience the same pain and trauma I endured as a child.

I didn't realize that holding this secret, although buried deep, was what led me to that place – a place of torment for me, a place of helplessness, and confusion for my husband.

At that first therapy appointment, I was encouraged to look positively to the future—something I had not done or considered for a very long time. Over the next few years, my Lord and Savior met me in my healing, and I've come to understand the truth of Jesus' words in John 10:10. He died so we may live, and not just live, but live abundantly.

If we are *content* to live in emotional or spiritual poverty, we deny the extreme suffering Christ endured to pay for our sin and Salvation. And that, my friend, is exactly where the enemy wants to keep you.

Thankfully, we have the power of Jesus Christ to pull us out of any lie Satan may whisper.

My desire is for you and me to honor Christ's death by living life to the fullest – **a life lived in abundance!**

Note to Reader: The end of each chapter contains a journaling page. If you need more space, there are extra journaling pages at the end of the book.

My Plan

God's Plan

SECTION 1

YOU ARE WORTHY.

I hope beautiful things

happen to you and

when they do, I hope

you can believe you are

worthy of every single

one of them.

–F. E. Marie

CHAPTER 1

Made for More

The waiting room was humming with movement—nurses in navy scrubs, techs in grey, a few doctors weaving through in street clothes. Everyone had a role, a rhythm, and a purpose to prepare him for surgery.

I sat alone in the pre-op area while my husband was having eye surgery. I was wearing a Christmas shirt that read *"The Weary World Rejoices."* I had opened my laptop to write—but I couldn't stop watching.

It struck me how much we rely on *outer layers* to tell the world who we are. Scrubs. Tags. Titles. Outfits. But none of it reveals what we carry beneath—the grief, the hope, the calling, and the questions. A reminder that our true identity isn't stitched on our clothing or defined by our job. It's woven into our spirit by the One who sees past every label. Our identity isn't in what we wear or what we do—but in *whom* we belong.

My husband came through surgery fine, and I came out of that pre-op room with a deeper awareness of my identity. If we have accepted Jesus Christ as our Lord and Savior, God adopts us as His own children, and we become heirs of His glory. (Roman 8:14-17)

This means our identity is a daughter of the King—adopted into His Kingdom, heir to all He has and most of all, saved from eternity in hell.

When God adopts us into His family, it isn't out of obligation. It's because He chose us. What we receive in return isn't just a new title. It's access to a whole new way of living. Once we surrender our earthly lives to Christ, we receive the greatest gift of all—eternity with our Heavenly Father. Christ's death on the cross wasn't only to get us into heaven; it was also about bringing heaven down to earth.

In the book of Luke, one of the disciples asked Jesus to teach them how to pray. Jesus then gave them what we refer to today as The Lord's Prayer—which includes the words, "Thy kingdom come, thy will be done, on earth as it is in heaven."

Jesus didn't die so we could just *get by*. He died so we could live—*really live*—with love, joy, peace, patience, and purpose. That is life in abundance—not a perfect life, but a full one. A life rooted in knowing we are deeply loved, fully accepted, and worthy of a life lived in abundance.

You were made for more than survival. You were created to live fully, deeply, and freely in the love of a God who doesn't change His mind about you.

You are fearfully and wonderfully made. You are His workmanship. You were created with a purpose. (Psalm 139:14, Ephesians 2:10)

So take a breath and engrave that truth in your heart and your mind.

What does God adopting us into a life of abundance mean? It means we are worthy to live in the fruit of the Spirit. (Galatians 5:22-23 ESV)

Specifically, a life of abundance looks like Love that overflows... Joy that isn't shaken by circumstances... Peace that quiets the storm inside... Patience when the waiting stretches long... Kindness that disarms... Goodness that reflects God's heart... Faithfulness in the unseen... Gentleness with ourselves and others... And Self-control that flows from knowing we are His. These things are ours when we live rooted in who we are in Christ.

As Christians, we are called to take up our cross daily and live exalted and victorious in the one who died for our sins. Being united with Christ in His death and resurrection is our identity...and that alone. However, we are human and make mistakes. We may think an abundant life grants us financial stability and loving relationships without conflict. We may also think it grants us accomplishments that fill our hearts with joy and satisfaction. But this is not the case.

We can live in abundance and face trials. Scripture tells us that we should count trials as joy, not because pain feels good, but because we know it's producing something eternal in us. (James 1:2–4)

Jesus Himself suffered. He was no stranger to sorrow. He uses the word WHEN in the verse mentioned previously— *when* you face trials, not *if.*

Therefore, we should expect suffering and trust God will use it to shape us into who He wants us to be.

So when trials come, don't assume you've failed, don't assume you are not worthy, and don't assume God doesn't see you. Don't assume you are not living in abundance. That's the mindset of living in abundance—not denying pain, but walking through it with Heaven's perspective, allowing the fruit of the Spirit to overflow even in the difficult moments.

During one of my darkest seasons, two people said something I'll never forget: *"When you love hard, you hurt hard."*

And they were right. I love hard—and when relationships fail, my heart hurts deeply. In past situations, I let the enemy pull me toward feelings of worthlessness, sadness, and spiraling into a deep sense of defeat. But our gracious God didn't leave me there. He began to show me how to live differently.

Two verses became lifelines:

Proverbs 4:23 — "Above all else, guard your heart, for everything you do flows from it."

Ephesians 6:12 — "We are not fighting against flesh and blood... but against the powers of this dark world."

These are also the two verses God put on my heart to write about almost twenty years ago!

Guarding our hearts doesn't mean shutting people out. It means filtering what we allow in—lies from the enemy, unkindness, criticism—even our own defeating self-talk. If we keep our eyes on Christ—*and what He's already done for us*—it keeps us focused on the truth. It allows us to guard our hearts and recognize where the lies or hurts are coming from.

Ephesians 6:12 reminds us that our enemy is the devil whispering comparison, insecurity, and shame; feeding us lies that we are not worthy of God's abundant love.

Here's an example of feeling unworthy of more.

In November 2017, my brother and I sat in the waiting room while our dad had quadruple bypass surgery. It would be a lengthy procedure, so my brother decided to go to the store.

I asked him to pick up a package of cheap Paper Mate brand mechanical pencils. Instead, he bought expensive ones. I was super excited but also felt guilty that he spent more money.

I felt unworthy of the expensive pencils because of the cost.

Later, I realized it wasn't about the pencils—it was about my heart. I had no idea how uncomfortable I would be receiving something better than I asked for.

But God used that tiny moment to remind me—*Stop settling. I've already paid the full price for you to receive the best.*

By the way, I never told my brother how much that moment stirred something in me. But since then, I've come to see that receiving something better doesn't mean I'm greedy—it means I'm loved.

Do you ever feel you are not worth the extra money, the extra attention, the extra love? That day in the waiting room, I was prepared to settle for less. But my brother chose better. He wanted me to have more.

That's exactly how God feels about you. Jesus didn't come so we could barely scrape by spiritually. He said, "I came that they may have life, and have it more abundantly." (John 10:10) That abundance is *Him*—His Spirit in us, His Word guiding us, and His love making us whole. Christ's death on the cross makes us worthy to seek and live out the fruit of the Spirit. Jesus says that He came to give people *life* in its fullness, not a life lived in emotional or spiritual poverty. His purpose is to give you a rich and satisfying life. Oh girl, don't you want a rich and satisfying life?

> "Above all else, guard your heart, for everything you do flows from it."
>
> Proverbs 4:23

Now, don't get me wrong—this book isn't about prosperity gospel thinking. Jesus didn't come to guarantee luxury cars and big houses.

He came to fill the *soul*.

He came so we could live with *peace when the storm hits, joy in the middle of pain*, and a sense of *purpose that carries us through even the hardest days.*

The Ragamuffin Gospel, a book by Brennan Manning helped me see God's grace differently. It opened my eyes to more of a spiritual side of understanding our worth, faith, salvation, and grace.

It's written for people who feel like they're never enough. The ones the church sometimes overlooks.

In the first chapter, he writes:

"Jesus is open with compassion. Something is radically wrong when the local church rejects a person accepted by Jesus... Jesus comes to the ungodly, even on Sunday mornings. His coming ends ungodliness and makes us worthy."

"Otherwise, we are establishing at the heart of Christianity an ungodly and unworthy preoccupation with works. Jesus sat down at a table with anyone who wanted to be present, including those who were banished from decent homes. In the sharing of a meal, they received consideration instead of the expected condemnation."

Amen and Amen!

That's the kind of grace I want us to walk in.

If Jesus says you're worthy... *what's stopping you from believing it?*

Take a moment. Pause and reflect on that thought.

Since our identity is in Jesus alone, we are worthy of living in abundance.

I've heard women described as "living life out loud." That's what I want for us on this journey—believing we are worthy of living life to the fullest, loving God, loving others, and yes, even learning to love ourselves. You are God's masterpiece. And He doesn't make junk!

My prayer is that you will stand firm in your identity. You will walk boldly in your calling, letting go of doubts, insecurities and unforgiveness that have held you back.

I pray you know this truth deep in your soul: *You are worthy. You are loved. You have purpose.* You are a daughter of the Most High King, and *you are worthy of all He has for you.*

Reflection

Christ's death on the cross makes you worthy to seek and live out the fruit of the Spirit. Jesus says that He came to give people *life* in its fullness, not a life lived in emotional or spiritual poverty. His purpose is to give you a rich and satisfying life. Oh girl, don't you want a rich and satisfying life?

You are God's masterpiece, created in Christ Jesus. Ephesians 2:10 NLT

Above all else, guard your heart, for everything you do flows from it. Proverbs 4:23

Moving Forward

How are you seeking the abundant life Christ died to give you?

Each day, look in the mirror and speak this truth: "You are worthy. You are loved. You have purpose."

Share with a trusted believer in Christ, your thoughts on how you can replace the lies you've believed with God's truth.

Abundance of your heart...

"Out of the abundance of the heart, the mouth speaks."
Luke 6:45

_____

_____

_____

_____

_____

_____

_____

_____

_____

_____

_____

_____

_____

_____

_____

_____

_____

_____

_____

_____

CHAPTER 2

Bought at a Price

During some of my most formative years, while I should have been enjoying the carefree joys of childhood, my mother suffered a nervous breakdown. My clearest memories from those years are of her either in the hospital or lying in bed. Out of respect, I won't share details. But I want you to know this: I watched God slowly heal my mother through her faith and the faith of our family. People who met her later couldn't believe she ever suffered from agoraphobia—a crippling anxiety that made her terrified of enclosed spaces, crowds, or any place she couldn't easily escape. But I remember.

As a teenager, I watched her rise from the ashes and fight her way back into a life of strength and abundance.

My father carried his own unresolved pain and expressed it through rage and anger. The stress of raising three children added to his struggles. Kind words from him were rare. He was a ladies' man, always chasing a dream, and never seemed to have time for his own children. In 28 years, I only remember one moment when I felt like he was proud of me. Once. In nearly three decades. As my father aged and remarried, he softened and even apologized for his way of parenting us.

During my mother's illness, when my parents couldn't meet our needs, the responsibility fell to other family members and friends.

It was during that vulnerable time that one man—trusted to help care for us—became my abuser. It wasn't a one-time occurrence; it happened often. With every instance, shame settled deeper into my bones. I believed my life was a mistake and I was a burden.

I built a wall. A wall of defense. A wall of protection.

I began to overeat, even as a child, thinking that if I made myself less attractive, maybe I would be safe. That wall of protection became a lifelong struggle with my weight–a battle that still whispers lies to me today.

Every extra pound became a physical reminder of the deep pain I'd hidden away…somewhere I didn't want to acknowledge.

When I finally sought counseling, I said through tears, "I just want to be normal."

My counselor gently asked, "What is normal? Describe that to me."

And I couldn't. But what I did know is that I had spent every waking moment since my earliest memories trying to prove I was enough. Perfection became a stronghold.

I strived to be the best at everything—card games, competitions, schoolwork, even being the first kindergartener to write to 100. I was exhausted by my own striving.

Desperately wanting joy, yet not knowing where or how to find it.

One early therapy assignment asked me to create a metaphor for how I saw myself. The comparison came quickly and hit painfully close to home. Actually, it scared me.

"...I felt like the brown paper bag you bring home from the grocery store. Once you pull out all the valuable items—the fruit, the dish soap, the essentials, the things that matter—you crumple up the bag and throw it away. That was me. The discarded sack. Worthless. Trash."

> Never take lightly the price Jesus paid for your salvation.

My own sense of worth was nonexistent. My insides were full of pain and embarrassment.

But Jesus didn't become flesh and suffer the full pains of humanity so I could feel like a worthless, discarded bag.

Today, because of God's relentless love, I can finally say I no longer feel like that crumpled brown paper sack. I am a radiant, sparkling, over-the-top beautiful gift bag, overflowing with His grace, filled with hope, and carrying the healing love of Christ to others. And friend, He can do the same for you, when you truly believe that you were bought with a price. (1 Corinthians 6:20)

The value, or price, of something is always determined by what someone is willing to pay for it.

And you, my dear friend, are priceless. Crucifixion was a death sentence, but it was also a public declaration of utter humiliation, reserved for the lowest of criminals. The Romans perfected it to break not just bodies, but spirits. Jesus, the blameless Lamb of God, endured this unimaginable torment...for you.

Never take lightly the price Jesus paid for your salvation. His suffering wasn't just physical–it was also emotional and spiritual. The agony He endured was the outward expression of an even greater suffering–the anguish of His soul, carrying the full weight of humanity so that we could be set free.

Jeremy Meyers writes powerfully about this on his website, jeremymyers.org. In an article entitled Crucifixion – The Physical Suffering of Jesus, he begins with this sobering reminder:

"I apologize in advance for the graphic nature of this post about the crucifixion of Jesus. We all know Jesus was crucified. But since nobody is crucified today, few of us realize how painful and gruesome crucifixion was. Two thousand years of separation has sanitized it. For example, if you do an image search for crucifixion, most of the images are pretty clean. It looks like Jesus stepped out of a shower, climbed up on the cross, and had some nails driven through his hands and feet...which hardly bled at all. If there's one thing we can thank Mel Gibson for, it's showing us the graphic and torturous nature of the crucifixion in his movie, The Passion of the Christ."

Jesus held the line for us. He endured every temptation, every insult, every ounce of suffering—because He obeyed the will of the Father and knew His death would have resurrection powers. While it's vital to remember the sacrifice Jesus made for our eternity, we must also never forget that He became flesh to walk out the full human experience. In doing so, He became more than a distant deity. He became a Savior who is relatable and near.

But why? Why would Jesus leave the glory of Heaven, endure unspeakable torment, and die for people who didn't yet know Him—people who might never know Him? Why would he come to serve others by sacrificing His own life? Matthew 20:28 is one of my absolute favorite scriptures: "Just as the Son of Man did not come to be served, but to serve, and to give his life as a ransom for many."

The answer is simple— Love.

Despite the redemption He provided for us, the world remains flawed. Things will never be perfect this side of eternity but we can rest in the assurance that God has a plan.

We can experience glimpses of heaven here on earth. The 'full life' Jesus spoke of isn't just eternal life—it's a life filled with purpose, radiant joy, deep love, pure peace, and the sweet fruit of the Spirit here and now. (Galatians 5:22–23)

So why, then, do we have moments where we feel anything but worthy?

Why did I find myself feeling like that crumpled brown paper bag? Because we're not home yet. This side of eternity is still scarred by sin.

And yet, "the Lord is close to the brokenhearted and saves those who are crushed in spirit." (Psalm 34:18)

I don't believe anyone else would be willing to suffer the way Christ did—let alone die for me and take my sins upon themselves. If our hearts are worth living for, and our hearts are worth dying for, then surely they are worth guarding.

Prayer

Father, I praise you for the suffering you endured to redeem me from sin and shame.

I ask You to break every chain that binds my heart—chains of shame, regret, and unworthiness. Fill me with Your abundant love and remind me daily that I am redeemed, restored, and destined for glory. Thank You for loving me enough to pay the ultimate price. Teach me to guard my heart fiercely, so that I may live a life worthy of the Gospel and flourish in the abundance of Your grace.

Reflection

Christ died so that we may live, and live in abundance. (John 10:10) Jesus walking on earth proves He was totally human. Jesus rising from the dead proves He is the Messiah and the Son of God.

Moving Forward

Ask God to shine His healing light in your heart and reveal any hidden places where lies reside. Do you need to accept, perhaps for the first time, that you are worthy of the love of God simply because He created you?

Share your faith journey with someone today. Your story could be the reminder they desperately need—that they, too, are worthy, loved, and created for a purpose.

Abundance of your heart...

"Out of the abundance of the heart, the mouth speaks."
Luke 6:45

CHAPTER 3

Guard and Protect

We must guard our hearts because we have a real enemy determined to steal the very gifts Christ died to give us. The attack didn't start with us—it began all the way back in the Garden of Eden.

Adam and Eve walked daily, face-to-face in communication with God, yet when the enemy approached Eve with a single, subtle question, "Did God really say…" she hesitated. That hesitation gave the enemy just enough room to slip in doubt. And she picked up that temptation and ate it like…well, forbidden fruit.

Fast forward to the New Testament, and we find Satan using the exact same tactic on Jesus in the wilderness. (Matthew 4:1-11) He tried again to instill doubt in God's promises. But this time, Jesus did what Adam and Eve didn't—He stood firm and used the Word of God as a weapon to defeat the enemy.

Now, fast forward to your life. The enemy's tactics haven't changed.

Think about those thoughts that seem to "mysteriously" show up in your mind—thoughts that question your worth, your purpose, your identity, and even God's love for you.

I'm not smart enough – Lie.

I'm not good enough – Lie.

I'm not beautiful enough – Lie.

I will never heal from the shame – Lie.

No one likes me – Lie.

I will never be able to forgive myself – Lie.

They can never forgive me – Lie.

If people knew my sin, they wouldn't love me – Lie.

I'll never achieve that goal – Lie.

One little sin won't hurt or lead to devastation – Lie.

Every single one of these is a direct assault on your heart and mind, strategically planted to erode your faith, your confidence, and the abundant life Jesus promised.

When we don't actively confront these lies, they take root. And once planted in the heart, they begin to shape how we live—leading us to act as if they're true, even though they are not.

> What enters your heart will shape your life.

This is why we're commanded to guard our hearts above all else. (Proverbs 4:23) Because what enters your heart will shape your life. And this isn't just personal—it's spiritual.

Ephesians 6:12 reminds us, "For our struggle is not against flesh and blood, but against the rulers, against the authorities, against the powers of this dark world and against the spiritual forces of evil in the heavenly realms."

Where are these "heavenly realms?" They are not some distant place far far away. No, they are right here on earth. They exist in our everyday lives, when you feel the presence of God, when the Holy Spirit intervenes on your behalf, and when Kingdom purposes are lived out.

Every day, we're walking through a spiritual battle we can't always see. Satan's army doesn't fight fair. He uses every weapon in his arsenal—sometimes even twisting the words and actions of good, godly people to inflict pain and keep us stuck in cycles of fear, shame, and doubt.

Levi Lusko, the founder and lead pastor of Fresh Life Church, describes spiritual warfare as "an all-out war going on around us—a war for our hearts, lives, and souls. But we can't see it because we have a blind spot."

That blind spot is dangerous. It's what allows sin to be a quiet, unnoticed foothold in our hearts. That's exactly where the enemy wants to keep it—hidden and undetected. Because as long as you don't recognize his influence, you'll never fight back.

But Jesus already showed us how to fight Satan and win! Recognize the lie! Speak the truth! Guard your heart!

Someone once asked Brennan Manning how he became an alcoholic, even after he was saved.

His answer was sobering and straightforward–"I took my eyes off Jesus."

That's really where it all starts, isn't it? The slow fade. The subtle shift. That's exactly what happened to Adam and Eve in the garden. They weren't overcome by some grand temptation or violent threat. It began with one single question from the enemy, "Did God really say..." And in that moment, Eve took her eyes off the God she knew and focused on the lie.

The enemy's tactics haven't changed. He still works to convince us that we're not enough by the world's impossible standards. If that doesn't work, he swings the attack in the opposite direction—whispering that we're more than enough all by ourselves, leading to pride. Either way, the goal is the same—to get our focus off Jesus.

I spent years, decades really, believing I wasn't enough. Not good enough. Not smart enough. Not...whatever "enough" was supposed to be. It wasn't until I was in my fifties, sitting in a counselor's office, that I uncovered a deep, hidden belief that had shaped my life. In addition to the lies of feeling unworthy and believing God had made a mistake, I found myself convinced that I was a failure.

Why did I believe that? Because I took to heart the words people spoke over me when I was young. I tried to live up to the standards set by a society that constantly moves the bar, a standard no one can attain.

Recently, while working on therapy homework, (Yes, I'm in therapy again!) I found myself back in the middle of those old wounds, face-to-face with the crushing power of words spoken by people I loved, admired, and desperately wanted to please, especially my father. Those words had become chains. As I was working through Alexia Folas' workbook, Triumph over Trauma, God placed these words in front of me: "We can often come to the end of our rope as humans. We face a 'Red Sea Moment,' where if God doesn't do something we do not know what we will do...this is where God meets us and we can overcome the devastation from the lies we believed, if we are willing to surrender fully to Him and His ways, He takes over and does more than we can ask, think or imagine."

"But God," I questioned, "do you not remember the deep pain caused by the words my earthly father said to me?"

A pain that, when remembered, shattered a newly broken heart—a heart so broken this time I was not sure even God could rescue me. At that moment, I felt God say, "But did He die for you?"

It took my breath away. Well, no, my earthly father didn't die for me. Before this moment, I never realized I wasn't letting Jesus' words carry more weight than the negative words spoken over me. This was the point I decided I would only believe what God says. His Word is truth and it is now written on the tablet of my heart.

This is why the enemy fights so hard to attack our minds through our hearts. Because the heart is the control center of our lives—not just the place we store emotions, but the core of our thoughts, desires, decisions, and beliefs.

In Hebrew, the word for heart (lev) speaks to this deep, inner center. That's why Scripture tells us to guard it above all else—because whatever rules our hearts will shape our lives. (Proverbs 4:23)

When Jesus said to love God with all your heart, soul, and strength, (Matthew 22:37) He led with the word heart for a reason. He didn't start with the mind or body. He started with the inner circle. To love God with all your heart must begin from the inside, not just through actions or beliefs, but with sincere, wholehearted devotion. To love God wholeheartedly means to give Him every part of who you are—your thoughts, choices, motives, and desires. As Colossians 3:23 says, "Whatever you do, work at it with all your heart, as working for the Lord." God doesn't want a piece of your life—He wants to be your everything; desired more than the air you breathe.

Just like an engine needs care and fuel, and a tree needs sun and water, your heart needs intentional care. Guard it well— because everything you do flows from it.

Pause, and think about this—the second half of Proverbs 4:23 says, "Everything you do flows from it."

Every decision, every yes or no, every word spoken, every action you take, starts with the condition of your heart. It is the most authentic part of you—the core of your being. It's where all your dreams, desires, secrets, passions and yes, even your fears take root. It's also the place where you connect most deeply with others and, more importantly, with God. And this is why guarding your heart isn't optional—it is essential for spiritual protection and growth.

When you recognize a lie and replace it with God's truth, the stronger you will stand. This is how you cultivate a heart aligned with faith and freedom.

Remember, Satan is so bold that he even tempted Jesus. If he was willing to tempt the Son of God, we can be sure he will tempt us. Matthew's Gospel details exactly how Satan attacked Jesus. In Matthew 3:16-17, Jesus experienced a powerful moment: "As soon as Jesus was baptized, He went up out of the water. At that moment, heaven was opened, and He saw the Spirit of God descending like a dove and alighting on him. And a voice from heaven said, 'This is my Son, whom I love; with Him I am well pleased.'"

But immediately after this, Matthew 4 begins with the Spirit leading Jesus into the wilderness, where He fasted for forty days and forty nights. It's there—when He was physically weak and hungry—that Satan came with his attacks.

Take note of Satan's strategy:

1. He attacked Jesus' identity: "If you are the Son of God, tell these stones to become bread." (Matthew 4:3)
2. He twisted God's Word: "Throw yourself down... for it is written..." (Matthew 4:6)
3. He offered other worldly rewards for worship: "All this I will give you if you will bow down and worship me." (Matthew 4:9)

Sound familiar? Satan tempts us when we're at our lowest, hungry, tired, discouraged, and distracted. Think about it, situations you handle with grace when you're rested and joyful can feel overwhelming when you're exhausted and depleted.

Using the same strategy, he attacks our identity, twists God's word, and offers us worldly rewards.

Jesus stood firm every time by declaring: "It is written..." He didn't fight Satan with emotion or willpower—He fought back with the Word of God. We need to do the same.

Revelation 12:11 tells us that Satan is defeated by the blood of the Lamb and the word of our testimony. In a courtroom, witnesses are called to testify about their experience or encounter with a situation. If you remember, in the Bible, there are many instances where witnesses were called to testify against Jesus. They were coaxed to tell lies. As Christians, Jesus calls us not only to provide verbal testimony on his behalf but to become living testimonies of all that He is and stands for. In John 13:35, Jesus tells his disciples that other people will know they are his disciples because of their love.

Living in a fallen world makes us vulnerable to the ways of the world: strife, anger, jealousy, greed, pride, and so on. But when we guard our hearts and submit to the authority of God, His Spirit will fill us with the abundant fruit that testifies of the change only He can create in someone's life.

Prayer

Father, I praise you for loving me. Open my eyes and my heart to wholeheartedly live a life committed to you. Forgive my unbelief and replace it with a faith deeper than I can imagine. Guard my heart and keep me close to You. Let my heart and my life be a reflection of Your love.

Reflection

Spend time daily reading and memorizing Scripture. God's Word is your strongest weapon.

If memorizing Scripture seems daunting, start small—one Scripture passage a week or even a month.

If you're struggling, don't isolate yourself. Seek wisdom from a pastor, counselor, or mentor who can help you see clearly and remind you of the truth you might have forgotten.

When you know God's Word, you can more easily discern His voice. (John 10:27)

Moving Forward

Share with a friend Scriptures that speak to your heart.

Write Scriptures on index cards, sticky notes, or whatever appeals to you, and place them where they'll remind you to live in abundance!

Abundance of your heart...

"Out of the abundance of the heart, the mouth speaks."
Luke 6:45

CHAPTER 4

Apple of His Eye

When someone refers to you as 'the apple of their eye,' they mean you are cherished above all others—precious, special, and deeply loved. It's a phrase we've heard often, but did you know this is one of the ways God describes you?

I was honestly surprised to find these very words in Scripture. I had no idea that God Himself says we are the apples of His eye.

Deuteronomy 32:9-11 tells us, "For the Lord's portion is His people, Jacob his allotted inheritance. In a desert land He found him, in a barren and howling waste. He shielded him and cared for him; He guarded him as the *apple of his eye*, like an eagle that stirs up its nest and hovers over its young, that spreads its wings to catch them and carries them aloft." (emphasis added)

Teresa Sherman, a woman God recently brought back into my life, shared a season of deep loneliness that revealed this truth in a powerful way.

After retiring from a high-travel career, Teresa looked forward to a new season of connection and freedom. Unfortunately, she retired just one week before COVID-19 shut down the world. Instead of new adventures, she found herself alone, isolated, and wandering through what felt like a personal wilderness.

With more time than ever, it was strangely hard to pray or open her Bible. One day out of sheer desperation, she cried out to God—in that moment of raw desperation, she experienced a divine encounter that forever changed her understanding of love. She heard two simple truths spoken directly to her heart—the Lord revealed these two things to her:

1. "Teresa, you know My grace is sufficient for you. But you need to know that My love is also sufficient. I am all you need."

2. "You are precious to Me. You are the apple of My eye."

She said the revelations "knocked her off her feet." In that quiet moment, surrounded by the stillness of her home, those words echoed louder than any crowd. They weren't just theological concepts or familiar Scriptures—they were living truths, breathed straight into the deepest places of her heart.

Hungry to understand the depth of what she had experienced, Teresa did what every searching heart should do—she turned to God's Word to confirm His voice and discover the fullness of what it means to be loved that deeply.

Teresa dove into Scripture to understand what those words really meant. What does it mean to be "the apple of God's eye"?

The 'apple' of the eye refers to the pupil—the very center of the eye, the part most carefully protected. Light passes into the pupil and is converted by the brain into three-dimensional images. But it's more than a technical reference. In Hebrew, the phrase means "little man" or "little daughter" of the eye — a reminder that when you're close enough to someone, you can literally see your reflection in their gaze. The pupil is also the most sensitive and vulnerable part of the eye, instinctively protected from harm. That's how fiercely God guards you—instinctively and lovingly.

Have you ever stood close enough to someone to see your reflection in their eyes? That's the picture Scripture paints—God is so close that your image is reflected in His gaze.

In Psalm 17:8, David pleads, "Keep me as the apple of Your eye; hide me in the shadow of Your wings." Just as a mother bird protects her young by covering them with her wings, David was seeking shelter in God. He wanted God to watch over him as one would a cherished child.

David wasn't asking timidly. He asked boldly because he knew he was loved. Even in his failures, even in his sin, David believed he was worthy of God's protection. And because of Jesus, we can stand before God with that same confidence.

Just as He did for Israel in the wilderness, God surrounds us with His presence. He provided manna from heaven, water from rocks, and complete protection from their enemies—even in the middle of their complaints and fears. And He still does this for us today.

If we're honest, most of us spend more time grumbling and doubting like the Israelites than we care to admit.

Do you remember these lyrics from a 1970s song: "You are the sunshine of my life, that's why I'll always be around. You are the apple of my eye; forever you'll stay in my heart..."

Do you know who sang it? Did you guess Stevie Wonder? I hope you sang it just now. What makes that song so powerful is that Stevie Wonder has been blind since infancy. He's never seen a sunrise, never gazed into another's eyes to see his reflection.

And yet, he sings about a love so strong it brings light to darkness. A love that opens the eyes of the heart and wipes away every tear.

Just as He did for Israel in the wilderness, God surrounds us with His presence.

What if that wasn't just a song about human love? Sometimes, even without knowing it, our hearts cry out for a love that only God can satisfy. Could it be that this song touched so many hearts because it echoed the eternal love we were created to know?" What if he was echoing the greatest love of all—the love of God?

Whenever you read the words, "apple of My eye" in Scripture, picture this: God, your loving Father, is leaning close. Your reflection is shining in His gaze. His full attention is given to you. You are precious to Him. You are cherished. You are worthy. And you were created for a glorious Kingdom purpose.

When we truly believe we're the apple of His eye, everything changes. Our faith grows stronger. Our hearts stay guarded against lies; we live from a place of spiritual abundance, not poverty.

Prayer

Father, I praise You for loving me as Your most cherished one. Forgive me for the times I've forgotten who I am in You. Open my eyes to see myself reflected in Your gaze. When I am tempted to believe lies—remind me that I am the apple of Your eye, fiercely protected and deeply loved.

Let Your love be the focus through which I see myself and others. May my life reflect Your glory and carry the fragrance of Your grace everywhere I go. Teach me to live boldly from this place of belonging, and to rest securely in the shadow of Your wings.

Reflection

The Lord delights in you... He will quiet you with His love, He will rejoice over you with singing." (Zephaniah 3:17)

Moving Forward

Look in the mirror and speak this truth aloud: "You are worthy. You are loved. You have purpose."

Ask God to reveal any area of your life where you are believing less about yourself. Where have you settled for less than the abundance He promised?

Abundance of your heart...

"Out of the abundance of the heart, the mouth speaks."
Luke 6:45

_____

_____

_____

_____

_____

_____

_____

_____

_____

_____

_____

_____

_____

_____

_____

_____

_____

_____

_____

_____

SECTION II

YOU ARE LOVED.

"The redemptive love

of Christ is why

we have salvation."

— *Vince Black*

CHAPTER 5

Lavish

This might be my favorite chapter in the entire book.

When I hear the words love, lavish, and heart something stirs deep within me. I'm not even sure why—maybe God planted this awareness in my spirit when I was a child, a small glimpse of the future healing He had waiting for me.

What I do know is this—God doesn't offer us leftovers. He doesn't make us jump through hoops or clean up our mess before we're worthy of His love. He simply lavishes it upon us. 1 John 3:1 says "See what great love the Father has lavished on us, that we should be called children of God! And that is what we are!"

The word lavish makes me think of soap or lotion being poured out, in excess. To be fully transparent here, I googled, "What does it mean to lavish love on someone?"

Answer: expressing deep affection and care through various actions and words, making them feel cherished and valued. That's exactly what I want to convey to you—you are cherished, loved and valued by God. One of the reasons I feel drawn to the words 'poured out' when I hear the word lavish is that it reminds me of the woman Scripture describes as "a sinful woman." She washed Jesus' feet, then anointed them with perfumed oil by breaking open an expensive alabaster jar, dried His holy feet with her hair, and kissed them. (Luke 7:36-38)

I am brought to tears every time I read, "a sinful woman" washed the feet of Jesus. She recognized Him and who He was prior to His impending death on the cross. With her one act, Jesus proclaimed, "Your sins have been forgiven." (Luke 7:48)

Don't you just want to sit and rest in those words? "Your sins are forgiven."

> What a difference it makes when I can start and end my day acknowledging His abundant love for me.

It took me years to learn how to sit and rest in God's word. But goodness, what a difference it makes when I can start and end my day acknowledging His abundant love for me. If we're honest, most of us don't know how to receive love freely—especially love that doesn't come with strings attached. Somewhere along the way, we picked up the belief that love has to be earned. We believe we have to prove ourselves first—clean up our mess, perform, achieve—and maybe then we will be worthy of love. I pray that by now, you have realized God desires to lavish His love on us as one more blessing in the gift of Salvation. So far, while reading this book, you've learned that being a child of God means you're entitled to every benefit that comes with that identity—

freedom, forgiveness, abundance, and a love that knows no limits. But, here's the question—Do you actually let God lavish His love on you? Do you sit still long enough to receive it? Do you stay busy because sitting still feels uncomfortable? Vulnerable?

When the noise quiets, you're left alone with your thoughts, doubts, and insecurities. Occasionally, it's easier to stay distracted than to face the aching places in your heart that wonder if you're really lovable at all. But here's the beautiful truth—God's love isn't a reward to be earned. It shows up in spite of your mess. It's present while you're still wondering if you deserve it.

When you stop striving and simply open your heart, you'll find His love has been waiting for us all along.

We're so used to constant noise, distractions, and striving that the simple act of resting in God's love feels... unnatural. But let me tell you—if you can quiet your heart, even for a few moments, and let His love wash over you, it will become one of the sweetest habits of your day.

If stillness feels hard in the moment, here are a few suggestions:

• Brain Dump—Write out every to-do list, every worry, every lingering thought on a scrap of paper, just clear the mental clutter.
• Play Worship Music—Let the lyrics wash over you and soften your heart towards God.

- Read Scripture—Focus on verses about His love and relish in the ways that God loves you.

Whatever it takes—just get still. Then ask God one simple question: "Lord, where do You want to lavish Your love on me today?"

It might be a breakthrough you've been praying for, an area where fear needs to be replaced with trust in God, or maybe it's the courage to believe you're worthy of love at all. The Lord is ready and waiting. His storehouses are overflowing. All you have to do is seek Him.

During my divorce, I moved to Arkansas to be near my daughter and her family. I didn't realize it at the time, but God had blessing after blessing waiting there for me. Now, I live just a mile from my favorite person in the whole world—my grandson.

Fellowship Fayetteville welcomed me with open arms. I found solid, Christ-centered preaching, joined a Bible study, and God led me to a small group of women who have become absolute treasures in my life and in a short time, we have developed deep friendships. These women are my people. But even with all these blessings, there were many moments of deep loneliness. People were busy living their lives, and I was still trying to find my place in a new town. And then, God sent Kristi.

She is part of my small group and needed a place to stay for a few months while her home was being remodeled. Without hesitation, I offered her my spare room.

She moved in on December 1st, and we became like two giggling schoolgirls—taking turns cooking dinner, watching movies, staying up late talking, and sharing life.

One day, a few weeks before Christmas, she asked, "Is your love language words of affirmation?"

"No, why?"

"Because you have Scripture and positive quotes all over your house!"

I explained those weren't decorations—they were survival tools. Little reminders to get me through each day.

She paused, then asked, "So, what is your love language?"

"That's easy," I smiled. "Quality time."

A few days later, Kristi told me, "I want to give you a gift that really speaks to you. Is there something you've been wanting to do but haven't because you're alone?"

Tears welled up in my eyes. "I want to go to the movies," I whispered. It might sound small, but to me it was overwhelming…I wanted to see a particular movie for weeks, but I didn't want to go alone.

We made a whole day of it—lunch, a movie, coffee afterward. I felt so loved! Seen. Cherished. Like I mattered.

That one experience changed the way I think about giving gifts forever.

Before Christmas, I asked my daughter and son-in-law what their love languages were. At first, they didn't know why I was asking. But when I explained that I wanted to give them a gift that would make them feel loved, they lit up.

Anthony wanted a tent with a built-in heater for winter camping. Maria wanted a new couch or a few home improvement projects completed. Since they have different love languages and could not agree on a single gift, I gave them a budget and told them to go shopping. Watching their faces light up brought me more joy than any gift I could have picked out on my own.

I had thought getting tickets to the University of Arkansas sporting events was Anthony's love language. I was wrong.

I learned something valuable that year—love is best expressed when it's spoken in the language the other person understands.

Just as Kristi blessed me in a way that spoke directly to my heart, God wants to bless you. He knows your love language because He created you. He's not stingy with His affection either—He is extravagant. His love flows freely, generously, and constantly.

Here are just a few of the ways God lavishes His love on us every day:

• **Unmerited Favor (Grace and Mercy)**
His Grace isn't something you earn. It's a gift freely given. His mercy wipes the slate clean every time you ask.

• **His Presence**
He lavishes love simply by being there—bringing comfort in chaos, peace in storms, guidance during challenging decisions, and courage when you're afraid.

• **The Beauty of Creation**
For me, it's deer—gentle, graceful, peaceful—a reminder of God's softness. Yet, they are also strong and powerful. In addition, the massive mountains speak to me as well—standing at the foot of the Rocky Mountains or the Grand Tetons, my heart whispers, "...Lord, how majestic is Your name in all the earth." (Psalm 8:9)

• **Community and Fellowship**
God's love flows through people, through family, friendships, and communities that uplift and encourage. Where would we be without the love of others? If you're like me, your favorite communities lead you to seek Christ in all situations.

• **His Word**
The Bible is God's love letter to us. It's alive and speaks directly to our situations. I'll never forget when a foreign exchange student staying with us read our family Bible and said, "How does your Bible know what I'm thinking?"

• **The Holy Spirit**
He is our counselor, comforter, and constant guide. He empowers us to love deeply, live freely, and walk confidently. When we don't even know how to pray, He intercedes for us.

• Jesus – The Ultimate Gift

God didn't just say He loves us—He proved it. He gave His only Son as the final, perfect sacrifice. And yes, He did die—for you too.

God loves you in the language you best understand, the one He gave you. His love is always more than enough. Often, the most lavish love is simply God inviting you to sit beside still waters and remember that He delights in you.

Prayer

Lord, I praise You for lavishing Your love on me—without limits, without hesitation, and without holding back. Your Word says You are Love, and everything You do flows from that perfect love.

Forgive me for the times I've turned away, believing I had to earn what You freely give.

Open my eyes to see every small and grand way You pour Your love over me—through grace, through joy, through the kindness of others, and through the beauty of creation. Lead me to fully embrace Your love, boldly, generously, and without fear of rejection.

Reflection

God desires to lavish His love on you. (1 John 3:1a)

Knowing your own love language helps you recognize how God is already loving you—and how you can love yourself and others deeply.

If you want to know more, you can take a free love language test at www.5lovelanguages.com.

Moving Forward

Look in the mirror and declare aloud: "You are worthy. You are loved. You have purpose."

Live daily expecting God to lavish His love on you.

Abundance of your heart...

"Out of the abundance of the heart, the mouth speaks."
Luke 6:45

_____

_____

_____

_____

_____

_____

_____

_____

_____

_____

_____

_____

_____

_____

_____

_____

_____

_____

_____

_____

CHAPTER 6

He Knows Your Name

Isaiah 42:12 says, "Let them give glory to the LORD and proclaim His praise in the islands." This is just what we did with IsleGo Missions. It was our second summer enduring miserable heat and working conditions in Steertown, Jamaica. These annual mission trips changed so many lives. During these trips, we built houses. Actually, to us as Americans, they were more like storage buildings.

Across the street from the mansions lived the poorest of the poor. The tiny blue houses are visible from every street in Steertown. These people have a view that the rich and famous pay millions to have. And yet, they live in extreme poverty, no home, no electricity, no food bank, and no medical care.

Our mission team loaded up every morning on a crowded, non-air-conditioned bus and headed out to hopefully make a difference in the lives of these people. As we approached the community center, the barefooted children chased the bus, hit the side and began cheering. In years past, we would all get off the bus at the community center, love on the kids and invite them to return for VBS.

However, this year, things changed. We were told to remain seated. As the bus stopped, my husband recognized a young boy from the year before.

Both of us had fallen in love with this child the previous year and our daughter had loved him from the year before that! We had pictures of this little Jamaican boy in our home and prayed for him regularly as we glanced at his sweet, tender face. If possible, we would have brought him to live with us. There was just something special about Conroy that tugged at our heartstrings.

> Jesus knows your name! It is written on the palm of His hand. *You are fearfully and wonderfully made!*
> Psalm 139:14

I was sitting on the bus praying for these children, wondering how our week with them was going to unfold. Looking up, I saw my husband getting off the bus. My thoughts raced from love and compassion for the children to "What is he doing? Why can't he follow the rules? Ugh, I wish he would just sit down!"

At that moment, I witnessed one of the most amazing events on earth. He stood with one foot on the first step of the bus and one foot inside the bus, stretched out his arms as far as possible. His posture reminded me of Jesus' arms in paintings. And he yelled, "Conroy!"

My eyes scanned this group of children, and there he was with a look that mere words can't explain. It was like Christmas morning, and he had seen Santa and all the gifts at the North Pole, or his birthday, and maybe even a day of reconciliation. Conroy smiled widely and questioned with wonder, "You know my name?"

Honestly, it seemed as if time slowed down. I looked at my husband, who was standing there with an expression like he had found a lost treasure. Then I found Conroy again, who was still in disbelief.

My eyes filled with tears, and I could feel every beat of my heart. Then, it happened! Dressed in old, mismatched, paint-stained clothes, sweat pouring down a makeup-free face, sitting in a crowded bus in a foreign country, hundreds of miles from home—I heard Jesus whisper, "Who is going to be surprised I know their name because you didn't tell them?"

Wow! What a shock. I was at a loss for words and just sat there taking in the moment. It was overwhelming to know that God saw me at that exact moment, and not only did He see me, but He also entrusted me with a responsibility I wasn't sure I was capable of achieving. I am constantly reminded that God doesn't call the equipped—He equips the called.

So, sweet friend, know this: Jesus knows your name! It is written on the palm of His hand.

You are fearfully and wonderfully made! (Psalm 139:14) You are deeply loved!

I've mentioned my precious grandson, who is currently seven years old. Like most kids, he sometimes forgets to use his inside voice when indoors, especially when trying to get someone's attention or asking someone to stop doing something.

Today, I want you to say loudly, "The Lord God Almighty created me. He knows my name. God loves me and sees me. His plans are to give me life in abundance. Thank you, Lord."

You may even want to write that down to reference whenever you need a reminder. Remember to say it out loud—use your outside voice! Take a stand! Praise God, thank Him, and your mind will thank your heart for it!

Prayer

Father God, I praise you because I am fearfully and wonderfully made. I thank You that You can use me, even in my worst moments. I thank You for knowing my name, which gives me confidence that I am not lost and wandering in this world without purpose. Thank you for revealing the power of my thoughts and words, so I can speak life into myself and others by guarding my heart, which affects my thoughts and actions.

Reflection

The Lord God Almighty knows your name. (Isaiah 43:1) Hallelujah!

God created you to live in abundance. (John 10:10)

Moving Forward

Guard your words. Choose one positive scripture or truth about yourself and post it where you'll see it multiple times a day. Speak it out loud every time you see it.

Be the voice for someone else. Text or call someone who needs encouragement today. Be the light that helps them believe again.

Practice every morning. For the next 7 days, begin your day using your outside voice to proclaim God's truth over your life!

Abundance of your heart...

"Out of the abundance of the heart, the mouth speaks."
Luke 6:45

CHAPTER 7

Jesus–The Greatest Friend

My dear friend, Pastor Brian Kimball, began a sermon with these words, "Jesus is a friend of sinners. He came to bring love and save our souls. He sought out the least, those with deep brokenness."

Imagine this scene—as the sun is rising, people begin gathering around Jesus, eager to hear His teaching. The atmosphere is full of peace from the listeners, but tension is also present from the Pharisees, who are plotting against Jesus. The Pharisees brought a woman caught in adultery before Jesus and the crowd. The gathering quickly goes from peaceful to confrontational. Jesus knew her sin and the law. This was a heinous offense, and the religious men demanded her death. Yet, Jesus said, "Let any one of you who is without sin be the first to throw a stone at her." (John 8:17)

> God loves me enough to call me His friend.

In her worst moment, she met the kindest, most faithful friend she'd ever known. That's the same Jesus who longs to be your friend. The same Jesus who already knows your sin and rather than condemnation, stands in your place. Let this truth settle deep into your heart: "God loves me enough to call me His friend." The God of the universe, Creator of heaven and earth, wants to be your friend and spend time with you. He loves you. He knows everything about you, including your darkest sin, and still says you are worthy of His love and friendship.

This longing for friendship isn't just for you—it was something Jesus Himself desired and modeled during His time on earth. I love the way Levi Lusko paraphrases Matthew 26:36-41 in his 40-Day Devotional, Take Your Life Back. "Jesus woke up his friends. He walked the ten paces to where the disciples were sleeping and said, in effect 'Hey, Peter! James! John! I'm scared right now and really alone. I have been praying, but could you maybe say a little prayer for me too?"

Lusko goes on to remind us how much power there is in having friends pray for you.

Have you ever been so overcome with emotion that you could not pray for yourself? I know I have had times of fear, times when I needed God to direct my path, and times when I needed others to help carry my burden. Prayer from trusted friends offers comfort, perspective, and spiritual strength, reminding you that you are not alone.

The Lord has graciously blessed me with many exceptional friends over the years.

There were those early friends who loved to skate when I was younger, providing a joyful escape from the difficulties at home. Teenage friends who shared fun high school experiences always bring fond memories. During my daughter's sports-playing days, the Lord provided an abundance of people who became more like family. Traveling all over Texas with the same group of girls and their parents will always be a highlight of raising my daughter.

As I think back on the people God has brought into my life, I realize I could go on and on. But one treasured relationship stands out as an example of the way God intended us to love one another.

God brought Deanna and me together almost thirty years ago through Moms in Prayer. One of the examples in Scripture of godly friendship that Moms in Prayer uses as a cornerstone is Mark 2:3-12. The passage describes how four friends each carried a corner of their paralyzed friend's mat to seek healing from Jesus. Because of the crowd, they were unable to reach Jesus. The men then cut an opening in the roof of the house where Jesus was and lowered their friend down on his mat. Deanna and I have carried our children and each other on mats countless times. She treats everyone she meets with kindness and a gentle spirit. We know the best about each other—and the worst. Our struggles aren't secrets. Praying together has bonded us in ways that words can't always express.

There are many ways I strive to be more like her—just like I strive to be more like Jesus.

Amazing friends are definitely one of the ways God expresses His love and kindness to us. Even when the world leaves you feeling alone or when you feel you have no community, remember, the Lord God is your friend. Take a moment as you read this prayer on the next page and let truth wash over you.

Prayer

Jesus knows me fully and loves me completely.

He calls me friend and I will walk in that truth.

When I feel alone, I will remember His nearness.

When I feel unworthy, I will remember The Cross.

I am never forgotten, I am always known.

My name is written on the palm of His hand.

I will live this day confident in His love,

and I will call Him my closest and most faithful friend.

Amen

Reflections

Jesus knows my name. He calls me His friend. I am worthy. I am loved. I have purpose. I am never alone.

Moving Forward

Find friends who point you towards Jesus.

Reach out to one friend today and remind them how much they mean to you—and take time to sit quietly with your greatest Friend, Jesus.

Abundance of your heart...

"Out of the abundance of the heart, the mouth speaks."
Luke 6:45

_____

_____

_____

_____

_____

_____

_____

_____

_____

_____

_____

_____

_____

_____

_____

_____

_____

_____

_____

_____

_____

CHAPTER 8

Love Your Neighbor
Love Yourself

"Love your neighbor as yourself" is a command we've heard countless times, yet hidden within those words is a profound truth we often overlook—the call to love ourselves. What does loving yourself look like in a world that pulls us in a thousand different directions, demanding our attention, care, and affection?

The commandments to love God and to love our neighbor (Matthew 22:37-39) are often seen as inseparable. Genuinely loving God leads to a love for others. When we express love for God, we recognize His love for us and others, leading us to act with love and kindness towards our neighbors. This automatically asks the question: Who is my neighbor?

Our neighbor is anyone we can share the love of God. We are called not only to love those who are similar to us in appearance or those we are comfortable with; we are to love everyone whom God places in our path or on our hearts. In fact, Jesus said, "I tell you, love your enemies and pray for those who persecute you, that you may be children of your Father in heaven...If you love those who love you, what reward will you get? Aren't even the tax collectors doing that?

If you greet only your own people, what are you doing more than others? Do not even pagans do that?"

God shows love to all people. As His children, we are called to do the same. (Matthew 5:44–48; John 3:16–18; Romans 1:19–20; 2 Peter 3:9; John 1:12) We are also called to love ourselves. Do you love yourself the same way you love your neighbor?

We are to love everyone whom God places in our path or on our hearts.

The truth is, without learning to love ourselves as Christ commands, we can never fully embrace the love we're meant to give or receive from others and from God.

What would it look like to treat yourself with the same grace, love, care, and kindness you are commanded to extend to those you love?

Before we can examine the way we love others, we must consider the way we love ourselves. If you think and speak of yourself negatively, you are not loving yourself the way Christ intended. God says you are more than enough. You are fearfully and wonderfully made. You were created as His masterpiece. You were bought at a price. We must let the meditation of our hearts believe that!

Dr. Caroline Leaf, a Christian cognitive neuroscientist with a Ph.D. in Communication Pathology, says, "If you knew how powerful your thoughts were, you would never have another negative one."

To love yourself the way Christ intends means to see yourself through His eyes—anchored in truth, grace, and purpose. It's not rooted in pride or self-centeredness, but in understanding your worth as someone created in God's image and redeemed by His sacrifice.

Christ's love is unconditional, sacrificial, and healing. Loving yourself like He desires means embracing His love without shame, letting His love define you more than your flaws, failures, or the opinions of others. It means forgiving yourself as He forgives you, speaking life and truth over your identity, and caring for your heart, body, and mind as a temple of the Holy Spirit.

It also means living with the understanding that you are chosen, cherished, and called. When you love yourself the way Christ intended, you are free to love others without fear or comparison, and you love from a place of secure, Christ-centered confidence and abundance.

Prayer

Father, I praise You because You are Love. Love is the very essence of Your being. Forgive me for not loving You, others, or myself the way You desire. Thank You for loving me, especially in the times I have not loved myself. Teach me to love myself and others the way You desire.

Reflection

Without learning to love ourselves as Christ commands, we can never fully embrace the love we're meant to give or receive from others and God.

"If you knew how powerful your thoughts were, you would never have another negative one." -Dr. Caroline Leaf

Moving Forward

Scripture says that love is patient and kind. Pray for wisdom to learn to speak and think of yourself and others with patience and kindness.

Abundance of your heart...

"Out of the abundance of the heart, the mouth speaks."
Luke 6:45

_____

_____

_____

_____

_____

_____

_____

_____

_____

_____

_____

_____

_____

_____

_____

_____

_____

SECTION III

POWER.

The Power of the Gospel
transforms us.

—*Unknown*

CHAPTER 9

Power of the Cross

God gives us power to use for His glory. Consider Philippians 4:19, "My God will meet all your needs according to the riches of His glory in Christ Jesus." Are you ready to draw a line in the sand? A blood line, if you will? Call upon the name of Jesus, the name that holds the most power.

When you recognize and understand the power you have in Christ, lies lose their grip.

You are equipped with the Word of God, the armor of faith, and the presence of the Holy Spirit. Nothing is more powerful! You do not have to live in fear, doubt, or insecurity. You have been given authority over everything.

Often, we forget that God's army surrounds and protects us. If we could only see into the spiritual realm, as Elisha's servant did in 2 Kings 6, we'd know, "Those who are with us are more than those who are with them."

The prophet Elisha and his servant were surrounded by a fierce enemy army. The servant panicked, but Elisha remained calm. Why? Because he could see something his servant could not.

Elisha prayed, "Open his eyes, Lord, so that he may see."

And suddenly, the servant's spiritual eyes were opened. He looked up and saw that the hills were full of horses and chariots of fire—God's heavenly army, standing guard. In that instance, the servant could see God's power at work.

Sister, this is your promise too. You may feel surrounded by fear, anxiety, spiritual attack, or overwhelming pressure. But your heavenly Father is not pacing in heaven. He has already commanded His army concerning you. You are never alone.

You are not just a woman trying to survive in a broken world. You are the daughter of the King of Kings—the One who created the universe, commands angel armies, and calls you His own. You've been chosen, adopted, and seated in heavenly places with Christ Jesus. That identity comes with power—not worldly power—divine authority.

When you embrace your identity as a daughter of the King, shame loses its grip and fear loses its power. You stop believing lies about your worth and start walking in the truth that you are fearfully and wonderfully made. (Psalm 139:14) Your Father delights in you. He equips you. He calls you to stand firm in that identity — even when the world tries to strip it away.

Jesus said in Luke 10:19, "I have given you authority… to overcome all the power of the enemy." Not some. Not most. ALL. That means you don't have to live intimidated by spiritual opposition. Yes, the enemy will try to lie, steal, and destroy—but you have the name of Jesus. The name that breaks chains.

Living in Kingdom power means you're rooted in truth, bold in prayer, and clothed in armor. Ephesians 6:10-11 reminds us, "Be strong in the Lord and in His mighty power. Put on the full armor of God so that you can take your stand against the devil's schemes."

Power as a daughter of the King doesn't come from striving—it comes from surrendering yourself to Him. It comes from being filled with the Spirit, from knowing the Word, and from standing in the authority Jesus gave you.

Just as Levi Lusko explains, "You may not be happy with your story right now. You may be disappointed or grieving or bored, or maybe you've forgotten you're living a story at all. But you are…with faith as your lens, I guarantee that what you are going to see will blow your mind. It's going to show you that you can reach out and take back your life from whatever is sucking it away behind the scenes."

When I read Levi's words, my heart screamed, "Yes! That's what I want people to know."

A woman living in abundance doesn't just see with her natural eyes—she learns to trust what God reveals in the spirit. She sees truth beyond circumstances, and that vision gives her courage.

She no longer cries, "I'm surrounded!" She proclaims, "Those who are with me are more than those against me."

Courage is something I truly desire, the same type of courage described in Acts 4:13, "When they saw the courage of Peter and John and realized they were unschooled, ordinary men, they were astonished and they took note that these men had been with Jesus." I pray that as you and I spend time in the Word of God and listen to His voice, He will fill our hearts with the courage needed to withstand the schemes of the devil and love others like He commands.

I pray that as you and I spend time in the Word of God and listen to His voice, He will fill our hearts with the courage needed to withstand the schemes of the devil and love others like He commands.

Jesus said in John 16:33, "In this world, you will have trouble. But take heart! I have overcome the world."

When your spiritual eyes are opened and your heart is full of courage and love, the enemy takes up much less time in your thoughts. You start lifting your eyes to the One who already won the war. If your heart feels weary, ask God to open your eyes. Ask Him to help you see through His perspective of love, His power, and His promises. Remember. Heaven's army is backing you.

This power isn't something you have to earn. It's already been given.

When Jesus said, "It is finished," He meant it. (John 19:30) The debt was paid. The veil was torn. Access was granted. Paul writes in Ephesians 1:19-20, that the same power that raised Jesus from the dead is the same power we receive when Christ died on the cross. This sounds impossible, but it is true and it changes everything.

Through the Holy Spirit, we have been given authority and power to overcome evil, to speak life over ourselves and others, and to live in abundance.

You are worthy. You are loved. You have purpose. When you fill your heart with this truth, your words and your life begin to reflect the power of His Kingdom.

Prayer

God use me to do the impossible. Give me a faith so strong that when the enemy attacks, I know I am protected because Your army of horses and chariots surround me. May I take assurance in the fact that victory is mine through the powerful name of Jesus. Open the spiritual eyes of my heart! Let me boldly recognize the strength I have as a daughter of the King. Help me recognize and denounce Satan's lies. Strengthen me to walk out of the burdens or strongholds so I may experience a life of abundance! Let me look back at the end of my life and say, "Man, what a joyous journey God took me on."

Reflection

If we truly understood the power granted to us through Jesus' death and resurrection, we would overcome the obstacles to living in abundance much more quickly.

Moving Forward

Spend time with God daily, seeking where He would have you walk in courage, acknowledging that you are not alone and that His angel armies are with you.

Abundance of your heart…

"Out of the abundance of the heart, the mouth speaks."
Luke 6:45

CHAPTER 10

Power in the Spirit

"But you will receive power when the Holy Spirit comes on you; and you will be my witnesses in Jerusalem, and in all Judea and Samaria, and to the ends of the earth" Acts 1:8.

Living in abundance is experiencing the work of the Holy Spirit in all seasons of life. The Holy Spirit gives us powers that are listed in Galatians as the Fruit of the Spirit. To access the full potential of this fruit, we must first exercise forgiveness.

As I've been working on this book, I've been reminded that the fruit of the Spirit is always available to us—love, joy, peace, patience, kindness, goodness, faithfulness, gentleness, and self-control. (Galatians 5:22-23) God never withholds these from His children.

It's like the analogy of what's in your cup is what spills out. When our heart is hard or restricted by unforgiveness, our patience wears thin, our joy feels distant, and our self-control slips away. The fruit is still ours in Christ, but unforgiveness hinders us from experiencing it fully.

I understand the importance of forgiveness and have witnessed people live joyfully despite their past terrible circumstances. I've also known people who lived enslaved to anger, bitterness and jealousy as a result of unforgiveness.

Forgiveness

Christ forgave us and surrendered His life. Who are we not to forgive?

Forgiveness is power. It breaks chains. It silences the enemy. It brings joy. Forgiveness doesn't excuse what happened, and it most certainly does not mean restoration will ever take place. Restoration takes time and a new sense of trust.

Forgiveness may not erase the pain, but it frees you from being tethered to it. As a daughter of the King, you were never meant to live in chains or under strongholds. The physical stakes are high. Holding onto anger and resentment can lead to chronic stress, which can negatively affect the immune system.

> Forgiveness is power. It breaks chains. It silences the enemy. It brings joy.

According to the MD Anderson Cancer Center website, "practicing forgiveness can reduce stress, anxiety, and depression. It improves sleep, strengthens relationships, enhances coping mechanisms and promotes healing and overall well-being—even in the midst of illness. Forgiveness can positively impact a patient's outcomes and quality of life during a challenging time.

Holding onto anger and resentment can negatively affect the immune system and treatment response. Forgiveness helps release this burden, promoting relaxation and better coping mechanisms."

Living in a sinful world, horrible things happen. I realize saying 'you need to forgive' is much easier said than done. I encourage you to pray and reach out to someone you trust and seek wisdom from the Holy Spirit.

When you forgive, you take back your power. You trade bitterness for joy and peace. This sounds exactly like a component of living in abundance.

Forgiveness sets us free! Forgiveness does not mean condoning or excusing the wrongful behavior of others, nor does it imply forgetting the wrongdoing. Instead, forgiveness is about releasing negative emotions and finding a way to move forward from the hurtful experience.

It is a powerful process that benefits us both individually and collectively, positively impacting relationships and cultures. Forgiveness leads to better emotional, physical, and social outcomes, making it a valuable practice for personal growth and well-being.

Forgiveness grants you power, and by default, love and joy.

Power of Love

The love described as a fruit of the Spirit in Galatians 5:22 is not ordinary love—it's Spirit-empowered love that goes far beyond emotion or affection for others.

The fruit of the Spirit starts with love because it's the foundation from which all the other fruits grow. Spiritual love (agape in Greek) is selfless, sacrificial, and unconditional. It flows from a heart transformed by God and empowered by the Holy Spirit. That makes it incredibly powerful—because it reflects the very nature of God Himself. (1 John 4:8)

This kind of love moves us to forgive when it's hard, to serve without recognition, and to pursue peace in the middle of conflict. It can change lives. When we love like Christ, we bring heaven's power into earthly situations.

A love created by the Spirit overflows into our daily lives, allowing others to see Jesus through us and in the way we live. It also has the power to anchor our identity. When we know we are loved by God, we no longer strive for man's approval or live in fear of rejection. We begin to live with boldness, confidence, and freedom, all leading to a life of abundance.

Power of Joy

Power can look like joy. Joy is not fleeting happiness that depends on circumstances, but a steady, unwavering state of mind that is rooted in faith and spiritual truths. It's the kind of power that endures the storm because it's anchored in the One who never changes. Nehemiah 8:10 reminds us, "Do not grieve, for the joy of the Lord is your strength." It declares, "I will praise my way through this."

Joy is hope in action—a bold reminder that God is still good, even when life is hard.

While Joy gives strength, it also brings hope. It lifts your eyes to see beyond what is and believe in what is to come. It opens your heart to expect the miraculous and reminds your soul that God is near. A joyful daughter is a powerful daughter because she carries the evidence of His presence and the assurance of His faithfulness wherever she goes.

When you choose joy, you are choosing to trust God's goodness even when you don't understand His plan. That choice makes you dangerous to the enemy. It fosters a deep-seated faith that is not easily shaken by trials.

Joy keeps you going. It lifts your head. It opens your heart. It makes room for miracles.

Power of Peace

One of the most comforting forms of power you will carry as a daughter of the King is peace. A state of mind that is not just the absence of conflict, but the deep, unwavering kind of peace that comes from trusting God in the middle of chaos. Jesus said in John 14:27, "Peace I leave with you; my peace I give you. I do not give to you as the world gives. Do not let your hearts be troubled and do not be afraid."

When you walk in peace, you are declaring that God is in control and that no storm can steal your joy. This is a power that confuses the enemy. When everything around you is shaking and you remain steady, you are operating in divine peace.

Peace is definitely powerful. It guards your heart, your mind, and your hope. It helps you hold your tongue when anger wants to speak. It lets you rest when anxiety wants to run wild. It lets you worship when your circumstances scream worry. Philippians 4:7 says, "And the peace of God, which transcends all understanding, will guard your hearts and your minds in Christ Jesus."

Peace is a gift from God. As a daughter of the King, you bring peace with you into every room, and you shift the atmosphere.

Power in Patience & Long Suffering

When patience and long-suffering work together, there is a quiet, steady kind of power that enables us to endure hard things.

Patience is the ability to wait with grace, to hold steady when life doesn't happen at the pace we desire. (Unfortunately, this is not one of my greatest assets.) Long-suffering, on the other hand, is the endurance of hardship with a spirit that refuses to give in to bitterness. When these two are cultivated together, they form a powerful strength that helps carry us through trials. It also says we are trusting in God. It's choosing to keep showing up with grace, even when everything in you wants to give up.

I will be the first to admit that I had to learn how to live with patience and long-suffering while waiting on God to work out everything for good in a situation I thought was hopeless. My faith needed to be strong because it was indeed being tested. In the beginning, there were days I prayed every fifteen minutes, then a layer of pain was placed on top of the grief and my faith wavered. It came to a point, I had to decide—do I believe God and trust His word or not?

Although it was the hardest thing I've ever done, I'm thankful I learned to walk daily in my faith with patience and long-suffering.

Learning to walk in patience releases your timeline and embraces God's. When you walk patiently in long-suffering, you refuse to let hardship harden your heart. Together, they produce a spiritual grit that makes room for growth, healing, and deeper intimacy with God.

Many times, no one sees the suffering but God. These times of enduring trials with patience can produce some of the most powerful testimonies.

When you think about it, has there ever been a time your faith increased due to an easy season?

The power in patience and long-suffering lies in their ability to reflect the heart of Christ. He walked with love, knowing His earthly life would end in torment. Yet, He endured with compassion. He bore pain without retaliation. When we walk in these same fruits, we don't just survive difficulty—we become living proof that God's strength is made perfect in weakness.

Through our patient endurance, hope is increased, faith is refined, and lives are transformed.

Power in Kindness & Gentleness

Kindness added with gentleness can soften hardened hearts, bridge gaps, and create room for reconciliation. When the Holy Spirit cultivates kindness and gentleness in us, we become examples of the heart of Jesus. That kind of power—the kind that doesn't need to shout to be heard—is the kind of power that can change a heart, a home, a community and a nation.

There is undeniable strength in a heart that chooses kindness and gentleness in a world that often practices harshness, quick judgments, and self-protection. Kindness is love in action—it's choosing to extend grace, even when it's not deserved. Gentleness is the posture of humility—it's a quiet strength wrapped in softness. Individually, each is a fruit

God desires for us, but when kindness and gentleness work together, they create a Spirit-filled power that can disarm anger, heal wounds, and draw hearts closer to God.

Power in Self-Control

Self-control, as a fruit of the Spirit, empowers us to say no to impulses, resist temptation, and live with discipline on purpose. Rather than being ruled by emotions, desires, or circumstances, Spirit-led self-control gives us the strength to respond with wisdom and grace. It creates space for peace, clarity, and freedom—freedom from regret, chaos, and the harm that comes from unchecked behavior. In choosing restraint, we gain strength. In surrendering control to the Spirit, we become more powerful—living not just by willpower, but by God's power within us.

Power in Prayer

When walking in the fruit of the Spirit, prayer, like forgiveness, keeps our eyes on Jesus and humbles our heart. Prayer is how we access heaven's power on earth. It's how we partner with God's heart. When we pray, God hears. When we knock, He opens. When we seek, we find.

There is great power in prayer. "Then you will call on me and come and pray to me, and I will listen to you." (Jeremiah 29:12-13)

I could write an entire book on prayers I've seen answered. Some of them are considered miracles. One of my favorite miracles involves one of my favorite people.

My mother was expecting her third child. However, at the three-month mark, she had not gained weight and did not have the normal belly bump. The doctor said the pregnancy wasn't viable and scheduled a termination for the next day. Our family and friends began to pray fervently. When my mother met with the Doctor the following morning, not only was there a strong heartbeat—she had a baby bump! That child, my sister Lisa, carried an anointing her whole life. She was a living testimony that prayer changes things.

Prayer

Lord, I praise You for who You are. May I take the following verses and write them on the tablet of my heart, for they reflect who You are and where our power actually comes from. Help me remember to walk in the power of these scriptures daily.

You will fill me with joy in your presence. Psalm 16:11

The joy of the Lord is your strength. Nehemiah 8:10

May the God of peace sanctify you through and through.
1 Thessalonians 5:2

He is patient with you, not wanting anyone to perish.
2 Peter 3:9

When the kindness and love of God our Savior appeared, He saved us. Titus 3:4-5

The Lord is good, a refuge in times of trouble. Nahum 1:7

Reflection

When we begin to believe the same Spirit who raised Jesus from the dead lives in us, we have power!

Moving Forward

Pray BOLDLY. God is still in the miracle business.

If you are not familiar with the fruit of the Spirit, I encourage you to read Galatians 5:22–23 and pray for God to reveal what He has for you in these Scriptures.

Abundance of your heart...

"Out of the abundance of the heart, the mouth speaks."
Luke 6:45

_____

_____

_____

_____

_____

_____

_____

_____

_____

_____

_____

_____

_____

_____

_____

_____

_____

_____

CHAPTER 11

The Power of Words

The power of talking to ourselves.

I heard the following story on the radio and had to go searching for it. Pete Weishaupt's website had an article that summed up the situation.

Trevor Moawad relayed a story—the article titled "Behavior Before Success" is a perfect example of how the words of our heart influence our mind, and then our mind influences our actions.

Here's some of the story…

"Out of the abundance of the heart, the mouth speaks."
Luke 6:45

"He graduates, attends community college, goes on to Wichita State, and eventually to an Ivy League. He goes on to become a successful magazine entrepreneur, but he didn't start on that path. He was running with the wrong crowd, skipping school, not doing his work, even talking about dropping out of school when his mom asked him to just do one thing for her—take the SAT test. He scored a resounding 1480. His life changed. He began attending class, he believed he was different and worthy of more."

"You think he's smart. He just needed the standardized test to unlock his potential. No. This isn't the story. What comes next is the important part. Twelve years later the man gets a letter in the mail from Princeton, New Jersey. He doesn't think anything about it. The next day his wife asks him if he's going to open the letter. He opens it. It turns out the SAT board periodically reviews their test taking procedures and policies. He was one of 13 people sent the wrong SAT score. His actual score was 740. People say his whole life changed when he got the 1480. What really happened is that his behavior changed. He started acting like a person with a 1480 and started doing what someone with a score like that does."

Moawad explains language is powerful, "but your behavior is way ahead of your success. The lesson is, in addition to language, how you feel about the past shouldn't determine who you are in the future. The keys are language and behavior."

He began to believe that he was a person capable of more because of the words he saw written about him. That's the power of a single belief. If a test score can change a life, imagine how much more the living, active Word of God can transform us when we truly believe what He says about us.

It doesn't have to be a profound life-changing moment. It can be as simple as saying affirming words to yourself. When my great niece was seven, she entered a local pageant and needed a sponsor.

We were frequent customers at a local nail salon and the owner was a close friend. I occasionally took Tara to treat her to a kid's mani/pedi.

One day, we were being pampered and Tara was going to ask Mrs. Lesley to sponsor her in the pageant. Tara had walked away from us, repeating to herself, "I can do this, I can ask her."

She asked, and of course, Mrs. Lesley said yes. Repeating "I can do this" to herself gave her confidence. I know that sounds simple, but she was speaking positive words to herself. (Side note, Little Miss Tara won her age division.)

Are your thoughts keeping you in bondage? I pray you will know you are made for more! You are made for abundance and you are made in the image of God to do great and mighty things. Believe it. Say it to yourself and say it out loud!

Luke 6:45 reminds us: "Out of the abundance of the heart, the mouth speaks."

That means that if you fill your mind and heart with the truth God says about you, that will eventually overflow into the words you say about yourself. When your heart is filled with the fruit of the Spirit—love, joy, peace, patience, kindness, goodness, faithfulness, gentleness, and self-control—your words become powerful weapons.

Do you love yourself enough to speak to yourself with kindness and love?

The power of words when God speaks to us.

The words with the most power are the words of God! In addition to hearing from God in Jamaica, I have heard His voice at other times—loud and clear. The voice wasn't audible, but I could make no mistake about it. It was God. His words were powerful. God can speak to you anywhere!

One morning at church, God spoke to me through a clock. Stay with me on this one. During a three-year adventure to Colorado, The Town Church in Fort Collins became a place of family.

Initially, services were held in a rented church building, which was quickly outgrown. An old school building was purchased. Until renovations could be completed, services were held in the gymnasium—a space without air conditioning. (Which initially scared this Texas girl!) The first day sitting in the new facility, I felt my attention being drawn to the sports clock on the wall, unable to look away for several minutes.

Each time I looked at the clock, God was reminding me that the time to share His Word is short. The clock remained a lightning bolt of conviction each time it came into view. It was easy to picture the clock moving, ticking away the precious moments in this game of life.

Prayer

Father, take every negative thought captive! Let my heart be full of Your word and Your love. Let my words, thoughts, and actions be a testament to Your glory and splendor. May I be a vessel of peace and a reflection of Your grace in this world. May I use the power and strength You have bestowed upon me to achieve what You have planned for me before time began!

Reflection

Out of the abundance of the heart, the mouth speaks. (Luke 6:45) That means that if you fill your mind and heart with the truth of God's word, you will overflow the truth to yourself and others.

Moving Forward

Let the following verse speak to your heart. Make a list of what these words speak to you and keep them close. "Finally, brothers and sisters, whatever is true, whatever is noble, whatever is right, whatever is pure, whatever is lovely, whatever is admirable—if anything is excellent or praiseworthy—think about such things" Philippians 4:8.

Abundance of your heart...

"Out of the abundance of the heart, the mouth speaks."
Luke 6:45

_____

_____

_____

_____

_____

_____

_____

_____

_____

_____

_____

_____

_____

_____

_____

_____

_____

_____

_____

SECTION IV

YOU HAVE PURPOSE

"God doesn't just call you

from something -

He calls you *to* something."

–*Rick Warren*

CHAPTER 12

Changing Directions

Generally, we think we know His purpose for us, but things can change in an instant. We may even lose sight of what we thought our purpose was. I realize now that the delay with the writing of this book was part of His plan. God had more situations for me to experience so I would be shaped into the woman I am today.

I am no longer a wife, I no longer have a 9-5 job, and I no longer need to 'parent' my child on a daily basis because she is grown and has a child of her own. God allowed each of these roles in my life for a season. Each role had a purpose. Each ending made space for a new beginning.

> God has a way of changing our trajectory to fulfil His purpose for us.

God has a way of changing our trajectory to fulfil His purpose for us. Just because your path changes doesn't mean you've missed your calling. It might mean you're finally stepping into it. If you feel God calling you to help in a certain area, you don't need to reinvent the wheel—find where He's already working and join Him! Let your availability become your obedience.

The following are real-life stories of how God redirected people, revealing His deeper purposes.

***

Bart Millard

If you listen to Christian music at all, you have no doubt heard the song written and performed by Bart Millard, lead singer for Mercy Me, "I Can Only Imagine." The road to Bart Millard's life as a Christian and the forgiveness he extended to his father is nothing short of a miracle. The writing and recording of this song is a perfect example of God having a purpose for every person's life, making drastic changes, and turning ashes to beauty. "I Can Only Imagine" catapulted MercyMe's band into stardom and made Bart Millard a household name.

But the success came at a price.

Bart had plans to play professional football. His father, Arthur Millard, was a local football hero in Greenville, Texas, and an All-American at Southern Methodist University. Bart's brother, Stephen, was also an outstanding football player. Everyone expected him to follow in their footsteps.

Then came a devastating injury. Two players hit Bart's ankles from different directions during a high school football scrimmage. Both his ankles were shattered—and so were his dreams of a football career. To meet Texas high school graduation requirements, Bart had to take an additional class.

The only elective that fit his schedule? Choir, of all things! It turned out to be God's divine setup.

Bart quickly realized he had a gift for singing. But his father, who had become emotionally unstable and abusive after a serious work injury, wasn't impressed. After the accident, Arthur Millard turned to alcohol and violence. The physical wounds were deep, but the emotional ones cut even deeper.

His father healed physically, but mentally, he was never the same. By the time Bart was 10, his mother had fled, leaving him and his brother behind to bear his dad's temper, and it was bad.

"He beat me three or four times a week," Millard says. When he was eight or nine, his dad beat him so badly that he couldn't wear clothes and had to miss two days of school. "I thought he was going to kill me."

One night, after an especially brutal beating, Arthur flipped on the lights and saw the damage he had inflicted on his son and broke down crying. "That's the first time I heard my dad cry," Millard said.

Bart didn't give up on his dad—and remarkably, Arthur found Christ. Father and son began to heal, rebuild, and grow close. Unfortunately, Arthur was already dying of cancer.

Even through the grief, Bart was amazed by the transformation. He finally had the dad he'd always longed for. That change became the seed of something powerful.

"If the gospel could change that guy," Millard thought, "the gospel can change anybody."

It didn't just change Arthur Millard's present; it changed his eternity.

At Arthur's gravesite, Bart's grandmother, who had a strong faith in Christ, said, "I can only imagine what Bub's seeing now." Those words stuck with Bart for years.

One day, they became lyrics. One day, when those lyrics hit the airwaves, they became a hit song. One day, they became a testimony that touched millions, and it arrived at just the right moment. When Author received his cancer diagnosis, he set up a fund for Bart to receive monthly checks for ten years. The last payment was received the same week "I can only Imagine" was released.

Bart would later write, "I know what I was before and what I am now. The only thing that explains it to me is Christ."

His story—the song, the suffering, the healing—was later turned into a movie, and Bart's memoir, I Can Only Imagine: A Memoir (2018), shares it all. A companion article titled "Bart Millard: 'I Can Only Imagine' Was Born From a Life of Abuse" by Jenny Rapson on ToSaveALife.com also offers an honest look into his journey.

His life is proof that God can use what the enemy meant for harm and turn it into glory.

***

Trish - My change of direction

A large portion of this book was written in a sweet coffee shop. One day, while I was there researching and writing, three young women were left to work alone without the owner. Their voices rose with giggles and chatter. One particular sentence took me back to my teenage memories.

"I don't want to have kids."

"What?" one asked. "Why?"

"Oh, if I find the right man, we might adopt but I'm not having kids of my own."

How many times had I said those same words? Growing up in trauma, burdened by a sense of guilt over my parents' divorce, (which I later realized wasn't true) I was determined not to bring an innocent child into the world that I didn't believe I could protect. I made sure my husband understood this before we married.

In the fall of 1989, I was working full-time, serving as a director for the Chamber of Commerce, taking three college night classes, and leading an exercise group. Life was full—and I thrived in that busyness. My husband was also in night school. One evening, he mentioned to a friend on campus that he was worried about me because I was consistently extra tired and had thrown up.

She immediately responded, "She's pregnant."

That night, we headed to Walmart after classes and confirmed it—I was pregnant.

My heart was changed forever. Our entire family fell in love with this gift from the Lord, even before she was born. I knew this child would be loved, and loved well! She is my greatest blessing. I read parenting books, took parenting classes, and prayed relentlessly. I didn't get it perfect, but I embraced motherhood and found immense joy in our little family.

Then God changed my direction again—this time through a youth basketball game.

At a Little Dribblers game, a few moms from my daughter's class were talking about a prayer group. I asked to join. That one request altered the course of my life.

At the first Moms in Prayer meeting, we followed a four-step format:

Praise - Praising God for who He is

Confession - Silently confessing sin

Thanksgiving - Thanking Him for answered prayers

Intercession – Praying scripture over our children

On the first meeting day, I entered the room and saw familiar faces, Lisa, Vickie, Connie, and one or two more. They, along with moms I didn't know, greeted me with love and an excitement I couldn't really understand...until we began to pray.

The leader explained how we were going to pray in those four steps. Okay, that was different.

First, we began to read Scripture that identified an attribute of God. Then we began to praise Him in reference to the attribute. That first step only praised God, no requests for what He can do for us, only Praise for who He is. A calmness came over me.

Secondly, we silently confessed our sins. Wow, that felt good.

Next, thanking God for answered prayers was in order. I was in awe.

Lastly, we divided into groups of two or three and began praying scriptures over our children, children we didn't even know, the school, teachers, school bus drivers, cafeteria workers, custodians and the administration. You name it, we covered them in prayer. I have no idea what I prayed for my child that day.

The most amazing part was that there was no gossip, no talking—just praying for others with love!

The one hour I spent in Moms in Prayer became my favorite hour of the week. I would like to share a story of what we prayed on my very first day and how it glorified God. I have no idea who this girl was, and it doesn't matter; God knows. I pray that on the other side of this earth I will know her, because I think of her often even though I still don't know her name.

You see, there was a young girl expecting. My thoughts were so selfish!

But their prayers went something like this:

"Dear Lord, if she's in this situation, her home life may not be good. Please change it today and bless her."

"Yes, Lord, let the teachers and students be kind to her."

"Lord, may she find peace and rest at school."

"Give her the mental and physical strength to have this baby." That went on for a few minutes—then they began to pray for the baby.

Let me tell you right then and there, I was hooked! I had never experienced anything like this hour of prayer.

Decades later, I'm still part of a Moms in Prayer group. Their vision? That every school in the world would be covered in prayer.

There are groups for homeschoolers, college students, working mothers, children with special needs, grandmothers— even teachers. You'll be amazed by the answered prayers.

Moms in Prayer

If you are interested in finding or starting a group, please visit their website at momsinprayer.org.

I pray you will be blessed just by reading the answered prayers on their website.

***

Maria Sharp

Here's a little advice: encourage your children to work during college—even if it's just a part-time job or internship. Gaining work experience in their field is invaluable.

When our daughter graduated from high school, we had set aside enough money for her tuition and committed to covering room and board. (I drove the same car for thirteen years, we gave up vacations and didn't eat out.) We were serious about wanting her to have the best experience possible and focus on her studies.

And she did just that. She attended Texas A&M University and completed her degree in Economics, with a minor in Marketing, at the University of Arkansas—all without incurring debt. But there was a catch.

Despite the degree, she hadn't gained work experience or clarity on how she wanted to use her education. She had briefly considered teaching but wasn't keen on more school or certification requirements.

After graduation, she and her husband moved to Colorado, and she began job hunting. One listing caught her eye—a liaison role between the U.S. and a foreign missions organization that provided clean water to underserved communities. It sounded like a dream job.

She applied and quickly received an interview request from the CEO. They met at Panera, since the organization didn't have a formal office. That's when she learned the position required her to fundraise her own salary. At that stage of life, financial stability was a necessity.

The CEO saw this wasn't the right fit and asked, "If you could do anything, what would it be?"

"Eventually, I'd love to work in education."

He paused. "You need to talk to the principal at my kids' school. They're hiring."

Though she reminded him she wasn't certified to teach, he connected her anyway. Within days, she applied for a paraprofessional role, despite not knowing exactly what that meant.

She interviewed on Friday. Started on Monday. And found her calling. A few months later, she attended one of her students' football games. The boy's mother approached her and said, "This may sound strange, but you are here because I prayed for you."

Maria listened as the mom explained that her son had been ready to leave the school. They had pleaded with God to send someone who loved football and Jesus, someone who understood his personality and could help him finish well.

That "someone" was Maria.

At the end of that initial meeting with the CEO, he asked her where she found the job information. She told him on a job site.

He looked at her funny and said, "We do not post jobs for this organization on job sites."

Neither of them could find the job listing again. Only God.

Everything—the job listing that no longer existed, the redirected career path, the divine appointment with the CEO—was God orchestrating a change in direction.

Maria later paused teaching for a few years to stay home with her son. She returned with new passion and earned her teaching certificate. She loves teaching math. But more than that, she loves shaping students into kind, capable, compassionate people.

Oh, and that student she connected with in her first year of teaching, she had the absolute pleasure of attending his wedding years later.

God doesn't just shift our path—He ordains our careers. Often, it's in the unexpected detours that His purpose comes into sharpest focus. Do you believe you can achieve the things God has called you to do? Say out loud, "I am fearfully and wonderfully made. I will live for God and God alone. I am worthy. I am loved. I have purpose."

I pray that empowers you! You could even do a Wonder Woman pose while exclaiming it. Imagine how your thoughts and your days would improve if you used your outside voice every morning to praise God!

***

Prayer

Father, I praise you for your sovereignty. I know You have a plan and purpose for me. Forgive me for the times I doubted Your hand guiding my path. Give me confidence to see You in every twist and turn—even the ones I didn't ask for. I ask You to give me the strength to discern the truth and believe that when challenges come my way, I will walk in Your light and remember I have a purpose.

Reflection

Is God using this season to change your direction?

God says you are equipped. (2 Timothy 3:16-17)

Stay in the Word. Stay surrendered. God's not finished yet.

Moving Forward

Do you believe God has a purpose for you—even when life feels off course? If not, be honest with Him. Confess your doubt. Ask for mustard seed faith that moves mountains! Are you allowing fear or the opinions of others to silence your dreams?

Look in the mirror each morning and speak this truth: "You are worthy, you are loved, and you have purpose."

Abundance of your heart...

"Out of the abundance of the heart, the mouth speaks."
Luke 6:45

CHAPTER 13

Apple Seed to Apple Tree

Some seeds are planted in silence, long before we understand their purpose. That's how it began with Savanna.

God plants seeds in the hearts of some individuals early in their lives, nurturing them over time. This chapter was written by Savanna Maxton, who recognized a calling on her life from a young age.

I have known Savanna, her mother Kristi, and both of her grandmothers, Cindy Maxton and Denette Berry, for many years. Their friendship over time is a testament to what it means to be "framily"—a blend of friends and family that enriches our lives.

In appreciation of Savanna's willingness to share her story, I am proud to donate 10% of the book sales profits to Savanna Cares. I believe that by raising awareness of her ministry, we can expand her territory.

Savanna's Story

Written by Savanna Maxon

At age four, I had a mysterious love for Africa. One day, even as young as I was, God placed Africa in my heart without previous knowledge of it to prepare me for my future.

For years, everyone wondered why I talked about Africa, and no one knew what it meant until one day, when I was eight years old.

During the fall of third grade, I had the opportunity to participate in the children's choir performance at my church, which had songs from different countries around the world. At one of our practices, we were singing a song about the children of the world, and I began to shake and had an overwhelming feeling to start a charity to help some of those children. At that moment, I decided to ask the Lord what exactly I was supposed to do. Almost immediately, I knew that God was calling me to send care packages to children in need in Africa and I would call it Savanna Cares.

As soon as practice was over, I quickly went to tell my parents about what had happened, hoping we could get my charity started. While excited about what I was being called to, no one knew how we would make my charity a reality.

Only a few weeks later, after telling my choir teacher of my plans, she told me that she had a friend who was a missionary in Tanzania and would love for me to ship some bags to the children there. I was beyond excited to have my first opportunity to send care packages, so my parents and I got to work right away, preparing all the supplies that we needed.

We collected stuffed animals, colored pencils, water bottles, soap, shampoo, and many other items. It was clear throughout this process that God had His hand on it because within no time, everything we needed for the bags was donated to us, and we were able to ship them not long after.

A few months later, we received an email that the bags had finally made it, and we read a few stories about the children receiving each of their bags. My favorite was about a little boy who began jumping up and down when he saw that he had gotten a bag without even knowing that something was inside. So often, we tend to forget how blessed we truly are, and this boy was a perfect reminder of God's goodness and the importance of being grateful for everything we have.

The summer after I finished third grade, I went to church camp with my mom. One of the things I got to do while there was to choose an activity from a list. Without hesitation, I chose to take part in making scarves for women at a homeless shelter.

While everyone was working on the scarves, the woman leading the activity overheard me tell my mom that they would be perfect for my bags and came over to ask me about what I meant. After speaking with her for a while, she asked me to share my story with the pastor who was speaking at the camp.

A few hours later, I was able to talk to him, and he gave me an opportunity to share the vision of my charity on stage that night, as he was already going to speak about missions that night. I was overwhelmed with how God worked it together for me to be at that camp and share my charity with hundreds of other kids. After that trip, I was able to send bags multiple times to kids in Africa and Jamaica as well.

A few years later, when I was fourteen, the Lord made it possible for me to travel to Kenya, where I would get to hand deliver some of my bags. I never imagined how rewarding it would be to see the joy and gratitude on each child's face when they received their care package.

One of my favorite moments from that trip was when I got to see the impact that my bag had made on a little girl who had received it one year before. To give a little backstory for this: when I sent my first set of bags to Kenya, I received dozens of pictures back of the kids, but one of the little girls named Milkah quickly became my favorite and the face of my charity.

I never thought I would be able to meet her in person, but God had other plans. While on my trip to Kenya, I had an opportunity to serve in one of the schools there.

After a long day, my team and I went to take the kids to the bus to go home, and that's when I noticed a girl with a bag that looked exactly like my Savanna Cares bags.

I quickly ran up to her and realized that it was indeed my bag, and the girl was Milkah! In that moment, I felt overwhelmingly grateful for the perfect plan that God had and the ability to get to speak to the girl who had no idea the impact she had made on me.

A few days later on the trip, God gave me another chance to see the effect my charity had made on a child. While my team was out building bunk beds, some of us played games with the children in that community.

As I was running around with them, I saw a little boy who had on a bracelet that caught my eye since something like that is not available to them. I walked to him and asked to see his bracelet and that's when I realized it was a slap bracelet from one of the bags I had sent a couple of years before.

Once again, I was amazed at how God worked it out for me to see the boy, and I took the opportunity to give him a new bag. Since then, I have occasionally visited Kenya, happy to witness the joy my charity brings to the children.

Not long after my second trip, I got a message from the pastor I met at a children's camp, asking me to do a Ted Talk along with eleven others. I was extremely nervous thinking about what to say or present, but once I discovered I was the only teenager speaking, my fears spiked.

Despite my fears, I decided to put it in God's hands and prayed that it would all come together. Just as I had prayed, my TedTalk came together and I was able to speak to a crowd about my story and encouraged teenagers to be the change they desired to see in the world.

My talk is on YouTube and I pray it continues to reach those who need it most and inspire others to say yes to the will of

God for their lives. In March of last year, I got a text message from a girl who was going on a mission trip to Honduras and wanted to take some Savanna Cares bags in May.

I immediately said yes and began the process of collecting the items that I would need for 50 bags.

About a week after the first text, the girl messaged me and asked if she could pick up the bags the following week since they were leaving on the sixteenth.

Extremely confused, I texted her back, saying that I thought the bags didn't need to be ready until May. She quickly realized that when sending the first text, she had accidentally typed May instead of March and told me that I didn't have to send the bags because of the mistake.

Knowing I couldn't handle children not getting the bags, I told her that we would get them done within the week because I was confident God would make it happen. Just as I had thought, God made it happen, and in three short days, all fifty bags were prepared and ready to go to Honduras.

As I reflect on all that God has done for me and the many opportunities he has provided, I am overcome with awe. I am constantly reminded of Jeremiah 29:11, "For I know the plans I have for you, declares the Lord, plans to prosper you and not to harm you, plans to give you hope and a future."

My hope is that my story will inspire others to take that bold step and be the change in our world. As I get older, I continue to pray that the Lord will keep using me to serve His kingdom, and I cannot wait to see His plans for my life.

**

If you'd like more information or wish to donate to Savanna Cares, you can find the ministry on Facebook at Savanna Cares. (https://www.facebook.com/Savannacares) You may find Savanna's Ted Talk under *Be the Change*. Let's help Savanna grow her ministry beyond what she could ask or imagine!

Prayer

Lord, You are the Creator of my heart. You know the deepest desires and longings that reside within me. I praise You for the promise found in Psalm 37:4, which reminds us that as I delight myself in You, You will give me the desires of my heart.

I ask that You align my desires with Your will. Help me to seek You first in every aspect of my life. Teach me to trust in Your timing and plan, even when I feel impatient or uncertain. May my heart remain open to Your guidance, and may I find joy in this faith journey

Reflection

God fulfills the desire of your heart. (Psalm 37:4) Do you have a burning desire in your heart that you think is from God? What is stopping you from acting on it?

Moving Forward

We, as humans, sometimes feel *as good as dead*. I don't think it's just me. We believe God cannot use us because of our past or current situation.

Guess what? Scripture says Abraham was *as good as dead*, but God used him to father a nation. (Romans 4:9) We are never too young or too old to be used by God. I often wonder what God will do with you and me if we surrender to His will and live out the purpose for which we were created.

Abundance of your heart...

"Out of the abundance of the heart, the mouth speaks."
Luke 6:45

CHAPTER 14

Run in Your Own Lane

God created our bodies to work as He designed. Imagine what it would be like if we had six feet but only two legs. What would it be like if each of us had twenty fingers but only two hands?

I am pretty clumsy with the two feet and two legs I do have. I can't imagine doing life with six feet.

It's the same with our purpose. We are made in the image of Christ. Yet, we are different. God gives each one of us beautifully unique gifts, talents and personalities for His glory.

Our uniqueness helps us reach the people God has called us to reach. God has a purpose, or a lane for analogy purposes.

Jealousy was a strong emotion Satan used to lie to me. It was certainly a huge roadblock in my recovery and in believing I was made to live a life in abundance. God has a plan and a purpose for each of us—a plan not just to survive, but to truly live. I am guilty of thinking things like, "Well, if I had her figure, I could accomplish this or that, if I had her education, if I had her pedigree, if I had more money, if, if, if..." There are times we even act differently to try and impress the people we are around. And let me tell you, this is not anything new...it goes back as far as the days when Jesus walked the earth. In Galatians 2:11-12, Paul calls out Peter for hypocrisy. Peter was hesitant to live out his belief that salvation is by faith in Christ in front of the Gentiles. Paul was called to the Gentiles, but the other disciples were called to the Jews.

Scripture also references jealousy; look at Matthew 20:13-15. This is part of a parable referencing workers in a vineyard, where the landowner pays all the workers the same wage regardless of how long they worked. Some of the workers who worked longer hours became upset that all the workers were paid the same amount. Isn't that just like us? "That's not fair" is a common saying these days, especially among children. It gets under my skin. Maybe because I've been there and thought things were not fair, maybe because I see what's available to these children and seeing things as 'not fair' says to me they think what they have is not enough. Sound familiar?

The landowner in the scripture essentially said, "Is it not lawful for me to do what I will with my own?" Jealousy and resentment ensued. I don't think resentment ever took hold in my heart, but jealousy definitely did.

God spoke to me twice concerning jealousy and feeling like I didn't measure up.

Satan used my weight as a "hindrance" to making a difference in the world. One night, as I was lamenting about my weight—asking God, "Why haven't You changed this?

140

Why do I still look like this? How can You use me when I don't even feel like I fit in my own skin?"

He answered in love so strong, it silenced the lie.

"You can reach people that others cannot. I created you for a purpose. Your weight is not who you are."

It's not about the scale. It is about the calling. It is about the millions of women who've cried the same tears and believed the same lies—God was saying, "I choose you to reach them."

No, the struggle didn't magically vanish. Now, I fight it from a place of identity in Christ, and not insecurity. I still have moments. But I anchor myself to this truth—I am not my weight. I am not my flaws. I am a woman healing and seeking to fulfil the purpose for which I was created.

> You can reach people that others cannot. I created you for a purpose.

Driving Me Crazy

Growing up, I wanted to blend in and not draw attention to myself. Don't stand out. Don't be weird.

And then, God, with His insightful sense of humor, created my daughter, Maria!

She came into this world loud, bold, and gloriously unconcerned with what anyone thought. She wore basketball shorts and oversized hoodies like a uniform, breezing through middle school and high school as if being comfortable was part of the dress code. She couldn't have cared less about her hair— or fitting in. And when she got contacts? She bought one clear box and one blue box. Her eyes are green and she wore one of each, so it appeared she had one green eye and one blue eye. Who does that? Weird children. But, you know who else does that? Children who realize their identity is not in their appearance.

Back then, it drove me crazy. I pleaded with God to make her more like...me. I heard Him say, "I made her this way. She will be friends with those who need a friend." My prayers for her changed that day. I stopped praying for God to fix her, and I embraced her uniqueness. And wouldn't you know it? That bold girl with the hoodie and mismatched contacts became a middle school teacher—the very age she once stood out in. She loves her students with the same fierce, fearless love that once made me nervous.

God knew what He was doing all along.

She wasn't off track—she was running her own race.

No Higher Calling

"I always wished you were my mom."

Is there any greater compliment?

One of the most powerful examples of someone running faithfully in her God-given lane is a dear friend of mine.

The woman who received those words never thought she was enough—not as a parent, and not as someone who enhanced the lives of others. Her deepest desire was to be a stay-at-home mom. And yet, society sends mixed messages—if you stay home, you're wasting your potential; if you work, you're not present enough. She carried both accusations.

I know this woman, and I've witnessed her talents, her gifts, and her servant's heart.

She can cook gourmet meals that nourish the body and the soul. She can serve 15 women in her home and somehow make it feel intimate and peaceful. Her gifts for floral design and tablescaping are exquisite. She paints, she sews, and she encourages with quiet strength. But more than all that—she loves and serves God with her whole heart.

I met her through Moms In Prayer over 30 years ago. She has prayed for the schools, the children, the parents to be kind when grades come home, the health and work/life balance for teachers, the custodians, cafeteria workers and administration—lifting up the names of those who will never know she's part of the reason they got through the year. One of our favorite prayers is that children would not have a wounded spirit. The ripple effect of those prayers? Only Heaven knows.

More importantly, she raised her children to know and love Jesus. She paid attention not just to her children's academic progress or extracurriculars—but to the state of their hearts. And because of that attentiveness, her daughter's adult friend turned to her and said, "I always wished you were my mom."

No degree. No accolades. No social media following.

Just faithfulness.

Just love.

Just running in the lane God gave her.

In God's Kingdom, there is no higher calling.

I used to think we were all in one race, side by side, striving to get ahead. Now I see life more like a relay. We each have a baton, and we're called to carry it through our lane—then pass it on.

Some of us sprint. Some dance. Some walk comfortably with mismatched contacts. Some walk quietly and softly. Each of us carries a divine baton, crafted for the exact path God wrote into our story. When we stop envying other women's race, we finally learn to own ours and that's the best race of all.

Whether you're called to missions or motherhood, ministry or middle school teaching, floral design or finance, you are not less than. You don't need someone else's race, someone else's pace, or someone else's approval.

God handcrafted your lane, knowing exactly what the world would need from your obedience. He says you are worthy, you are loved, and you have purpose.

I pray you will run hard after your God-given calling—not with striving or fear, but with the joy of knowing He has supplied you with everything you need to finish strong. Keep the eyes of your heart open and run.

My encouragement to you is to run in your own lane and embrace the purpose God has for you.

We stumble when we don't run in our own lane. But more importantly, we may cause others to stumble when we try to crowd them out or share their lane. There's no room in your lane for others—and vice versa.

I pray you will run hard after your God given purpose! I pray you know He has supplied you with everything you need to accomplish that purpose. Keep the eyes of your heart open and run.

If possible, take a break from reading, grab your favorite coffee, tea, or water and sit with God. Share with Him your concerns, your questions, or just your thoughts. He already knows—but He still wants to hear from you.

Prayer

Father, I praise You for making me uniquely wonderful. I come before You with a heart full of gratitude for the gifts, strengths, and callings You've woven into my life. Thank You for shaping me in Your image, and I ask for the courage to embrace the lane You designed just for me.

Guard my heart from jealousy and comparison. Teach me to celebrate others without questioning my own worth. Help me see that I don't need to compete because I'm already complete in You.

Let my life be a reflection of Your love and glory—right here, right now, exactly where You've placed me.

Reflection

If you believe you deserve to live in spiritual, mental, or emotional poverty, then you're denying the very power of the Cross. Jesus didn't die for you to compare. He died for you to live—fully, freely, and fearlessly.

- God says you are made new. (2 Corinthians 5:17)
- God gives grace upon grace. (John 1:16)
- God set a race before you—and He's cheering you on.

So lace up. Lift your eyes. Run—not like you're behind—but with confidence knowing Heaven has already marked your finish line. The world needs what only you can bring.

Moving Forward

Lord, is there any jealousy, comparison, or discontent hiding in my heart?

Am I running in the lane you designed for me—or am I trying to merge into someone else's?

Abundance of your heart...

"Out of the abundance of the heart, the mouth speaks."
Luke 6:45

_____

_____

_____

_____

_____

_____

_____

_____

_____

_____

_____

_____

_____

_____

_____

_____

_____

_____

_____

CHAPTER 15

Fear and Unbelief

Fear and unbelief do more than hold you back—they can cripple the purpose God has called you to fulfill. Unbelief is something I can speak to firsthand, as I've struggled with it over the years. Occasionally, I have to remind myself: I am worthy of living a life full of love, joy, peace, patience, kindness, and goodness. There is purpose to be found even in patience and long-suffering.

I was surprised to read about this same type of unbelief from the early church in Acts 12:1-17. These verses convey to us how God miraculously freed Peter from prison.

King Herod began persecuting the church. He had James, the brother of John, executed, and when he saw how pleased the people were, he had Peter arrested—right during the Festival of Unleavened Bread. Peter was thrown into prison under heavy guard, with plans for a public trial after Passover. But while Peter was in prison, the church prayed earnestly for him. The night before his trial, Peter was sleeping between two soldiers, chained, with guards at the door. Suddenly, an angel appeared, lighting up the cell. He woke Peter, telling him to get up—and the chains fell off.

The angel told him to dress and follow. Peter, thinking it was all a vision, obeyed.

> God will use anybody who will trust Him and expect to be used by Him— not because of who you are but because it brings Him glory.
> – Rick Warren

They passed the guards and came to the iron gate, which opened on its own. After walking a street's length, the angel disappeared. Then Peter realized it was real—God had rescued him from Herod!

Peter went on to Mary's house, where many believers were praying. When he knocked, a servant girl recognized his voice and ran to tell the others, forgetting to open the door. They didn't believe her at first, and told her she was *out of her mind*. Peter kept knocking. The prayer warriors answered in unbelief—it couldn't be him because Peter was in prison.

Goodness, they were witnesses to a miracle. God answered their prayer in a miraculous way, in a way they didn't expect and they didn't believe! Don't we do the same thing? We pray without believing. God still performs miracles, even when we've found ourselves in unbelief.

God will use anybody who will trust Him and expect to be used by Him—not because of who you are but because it brings Him glory. – Rick Warren

Freedom from fear and unbelief is a gift God has given us so we can live in abundance. Let's break down that gift into four easy steps so we can utilize the G.I.F.T. each and every day.

G- Glorify God

In all circumstances, we should glorify God. We do this by reminding ourselves of who He is and what He has done in the past. When we reflect with gratitude and gratefulness, this minimizes fear and unbelief because it reminds us that if God was faithful once, surely He will be faithful again and again.

I- Identify Your Assets

Many times, fear can creep in when we are facing a difficult time or called beyond our comfort zone. Think about Peter walking on water. He stepped out of the boat and began walking to Jesus but lost sight of the Lord and began to sink. (Matthew 14:22-23) All Peter had at the time was faith in Jesus and his legs. He had seen Jesus perform miracles, so he knew if Jesus said "come," he could go. He used his legs to start the journey. He could have walked all the way to Jesus, but he began to doubt the power he had. Maybe faith wasn't enough.

Oh, Peter, that was a lie; you could have walked all the way.

Or, think of the widow in 2 Kings 4. Elisha asked, "What do you have in your house?" She was in a desperate situation, and he asked her to evaluate her assets. She had pots, and she had neighbors. The widow took her pots and the pots she had borrowed from neighbors, and she began pouring out oil until all the pots were full.

We may not think we have what it takes to complete the work God has called us to, but when we start with what we do have, God will fill the gap.

F- Filter out dream killers

Many times, our biggest mistake that causes fear and unbelief in our journey is sharing a dream with the wrong individual. I think about the story of Jarius in Mark 5. He was a synagogue leader with a very sick daughter. He had seen Jesus perform miracles and had faith that he could do the same for his daughter. As they were heading to his house, a servant found him and said, "Don't bother Jesus, your daughter is dead." If I were Jarius, I would have been devastated to hear this and may have allowed unbelief to rob me of my miracle. Thankfully, for Jarius, Jesus was right there with him and said, "Don't be afraid, just believe."

Protect the abundant life God has for you against fear and unbelief by guarding your hearts carefully and staying close to Jesus. Many times, we need to refrain from telling the masses our plans because the story is not meant to be shared until after the miracle is performed.

T- Trust God's Abundance

Lastly, to accept God's gift for us to live an abundant life, we must believe that He is trustworthy and faithful to deliver on what He has said. We see this kind of faith in David when he charged out to slay Goliath. David stormed the battlefield, shouting, "You come against me with sword and spear and javelin, but I come against you in the name of the LORD Almighty...This day the LORD will deliver you into my hands." 1 Samuel 17:45-46

David was surrounded by his countrymen, God's chosen people—Israel, who were shaking in fear and unbelief. They had seen God deliver them many times on the battlefield, but this time they were cowering in fear. David was the only one trusting in God's abundance that day. His trust in the Lord changed the fate of an entire nation.

There's a high cost to fear and unbelief. Not only will it rob our peace, but it will rob us of the fruit we're meant to bear. Don't let fear or unbelief rob you or others of joy and purpose. You were born to live a life of abundance. Belief and obedience to God could be the key that you, and others witnessing your walk, need to unlock breakthroughs, provide courage, and walk out your purpose with confidence and joy!

Prayer

Lord, You've been faithful before, and I know You'll be faithful again. I will not wait for perfect conditions, but I'll use the gifts and talents You've given me today. I will strengthen myself in You, not in the approval of others.

Jesus, take every part of my life and be Lord over it all. The battle is Yours, not mine.

I thank You in advance for the giants that will fall and the mountains that will be moved in Your name.

May Your name be glorified. Amen.

Hebrews 13:8, 1 Samuel 17:40, 1 Samuel 30:6, 2 Chronicles 20:15, Philippians 1:6

Reflection

Every task assigned by God carries a significant impact. Nothing is small when it comes to God. While at an "IF" conference, I heard Christine Caine say, "Someone prepared the 5 loaves and 2 fish Jesus used to feed the five thousand." Why is that significant?

God uses everything! Instead of thinking we have too little to "bring to the table" we need to bring what we do have and allow God to use it. When we doubt the significance of our gifts, our unbelief could be limiting others. This isn't to say that God would not still provide, but wouldn't you love to be part of His miracle?

Moving Forward

Contemplate what you have learned about yourself and fear. Move forward with courage, confidence and conviction.

What "giants" are standing between you and your dream or the purpose you feel called to walk in?

Think of the tools that God has given you to accomplish your task. How well are you using them?

How do you want to be used by God?

Do you expect him to do it?

Do you want the direction and protection that comes from being in a relationship with Jesus Christ?

You don't need to know what's going to happen tomorrow. You don't need to know what the future holds; you just need to know who holds the future! When you have a relationship with your Creator, you'll have the security of his unwavering love and unbreakable promises.

Prayer to Begin a Relationship with Jesus

Dear Jesus Christ, I want my security to rest in You and You alone. Today, I choose to claim the promise that You will never leave me or forsake me.

As much as I know how, I open my heart and my life to You, Lord Jesus. I confess that I have lived life my own way and sinned against You. Forgive me and wash me clean.

Come into my heart and my life, Lord, and make me new.

Change my priorities, my values, my purpose, and my direction. Transform me into the person You created me to be as I fully surrender to You.

I trust in You as my Lord and Savior, and I submit my life into Your hands.

In Jesus' name I pray. Amen.

Hebrews 13:5, Romans 3:23, 1 John 1:9, 2 Corinthians 5:17, Romans 12:1-2

Abundance of your heart...

"Out of the abundance of the heart, the mouth speaks."
Luke 6:45

_____

_____

_____

_____

_____

_____

_____

_____

_____

_____

_____

_____

_____

_____

_____

_____

_____

CONCLUSION

As you turn the final page, take a moment to reflect on how far God has brought you in this journey.

We began in the place of WORTH—remembering that you are Made for More, Bought at a Price, A Friend of Jesus and forever the Apple of His Eye. Jesus' death and resurrection define your worth.

Then, we moved into the embrace of His LOVE—you read that God desires to Lavish His love on you, He Knows Your Name, and is The Greatest Friend. I hope God allowed you to see yourself through His eyes and encouraged you to show others this same love—loving your neighbor as yourself.

After learning that the Lord deems you worthy and loved, we looked at your POWER—the indescribable power from The Cross, The Holy Spirit and Word of God. You also examined the power in your own thoughts and words.

From there, we stepped into PURPOSE—even when the path required Changing Directions, or possibly was instilled in you from Apple Seed to Apple Tree, you discovered that Running in Your Own Lane means trusting God with the assignment only you were created to fulfill. You have replaced Fear and Unbelief with Power and Purpose!

I am praying Habakkuk 1:5 from the Living Bible Translation over you. I cannot wait to hear how the Lord works in your life. Thank you for allowing me to share the window of my heart and you are now a part of my story. It humbles me that the Lord would use me to share His word to make a positive difference in your life.

So, as you close this book, don't rush. Pause. Grab your favorite coffee or tea, a writing tool, and maybe even a journal. Sit back and receive the love the Father has for you. Have a conversation with Him. Let Him love you. Ask Him, "How do You want me to live an abundant life that accomplishes Your purpose?"

"The Lord replied: Look, and be amazed!
You will be astounded at what I am about to do!
For I am going to do something in your own lifetime
that you will have to see to believe."

—Habakkuk 1:5

The Lord God Almighty,
Creator of heaven and earth, created you!

You are worthy.

You are loved.

You have purpose.

READING SUGGESTIONS

I Want to Trust You, But I Don't by Lysa TerKeurst

Take Back Your Life by Levi Lusko

Triumph over Trauma by Alexas Follas

Believing Jesus by Lisa Harper

Take Courage Bible Study by Jennifer Rothschild

I Can Only Imagine by Bart Millard and Robert Nolan

In a Pit with a Lion on a Snowy Day by Mark Batterson

Circle Maker by Mark Batterson

Win the Day by Mark Batterson

The Five Love Languages by Gary Chapman

David and Goliath by Malcolm Goldman

TED TALK SUGGESTIONS

Your body language may shape who you are - Amy Cuddy

Be the Change - Savanna Maxton

WORKS CITED

Take Back Your Life
by Levi Lusko

The Ragamuffin Gospel
by Brennan Manning

Crucifixion – The Physical Suffering of Jesus
by Jeremy Meyers, jeremymyers.org

Triumph over Trauma
by Alexia Folas

www.5lovelanguages.com

Switch on Your Brain
by Dr. Caroline Leaf

"Therapeutic Aspects of Clinician-Patient Relationships,"
presented by Dr. Dennis Novack.
streaming.mdanderson.org

"Behavior Before Success"
by Trevor Moaward
peteweishaupt.medium.com

I Can Only Imagine: A Memoir (2018) by Bart Millard
"Bart Millard: 'I Can Only Imagine' Was Born From a
Life of Abuse"
by Jenny Rapson, ToSaveALife.com

Momsinprayer.org

Notes to Live in Abundance

Notes to Live in Abundance

Notes to Live in Abundance

Notes to Live in Abundance

Notes to Live in Abundance

Notes to Live in Abundance

Notes to Live in Abundance

Notes to Live in Abundance

Notes to Live in Abundance

Notes to Live in Abundance

ABOUT THE AUTHOR

Trish Kuhl is an inspirational Christian author, speaker, and founder of Living in Abundance, devoted to helping women embrace the abundant life God promises through Jesus Christ.

Having once struggled with feelings of inadequacy, Trish encountered the redeeming love of Christ and discovered freedom, healing, and purpose in Him. Her heart is to help women know they are worthy, deeply loved, and created with purpose.

Trish shares her message through writing, speaking, and retreats that encourage women to walk boldly in their God-given identity and calling. She co-authored *Jingle Your Jolly* and is a contributing author to *Successful in His Eyes*.

Beyond ministry, Trish enjoys painting, photography, volunteering, and spending time outdoors. Her greatest joy is being "Mimi" to her beloved grandson, Isaiah.